DOWN SOUTH
PALEO

★ ★ ★

Delectable Southern Recipes
Adapted for Gluten-Free, Paleo Eaters

JENNIFER ROBINS

founder of the popular blog Predominantly Paleo

PAGE STREET
PUBLISHING CO.

PAGE STREET
PUBLISHING CO.

Distributed by Macmillan; sales in Canada by The Canadian Manda Group

18 17 16 15   3 4 5 6

ISBN-13: 978-1-62414-132-4
ISBN-10: 1-62414-132-3

Library of Congress Control Number: 2015930604

Cover and book design by Page Street Publishing Co.
Photography by Stephanie Gaudreau

Printed and bound in U.S.A.

Page Street is proud to be a member of 1% for the Planet. Members donate one percent of their
sales to one or more of the over 1,500 environmental and sustainability charities across the globe
who participate in this program.

TO MY LITTLE ROBINS NEST,
THANKS FOR HELPING ME
LEARN TO FLY
ALL OVER AGAIN.

★ ★ ★

CONTENTS

★ ★ ★

ON THE SIDE | 91

FOREWORD

★ ★ ★

Y'all listen up now. If you're not already in love with Jennifer's food, her welcoming smile and Southern charm—well then, bless your heart because I'm here to tell you it's time! I've had the pleasure of knowing Jennifer for years, and loving her food for just as long! As a friend with experience writing cookbooks, I had the good fortune of talking with Jen as she worked busy as a cat on a hot tin roof pulling this book together. But even knowing all that went into it along the way, I was blown away by the end result.

After my own experiences running a blog and writing several cookbooks, I know first-hand how difficult it is to recreate recipes that people associate with memories, classics passed down generation after generation. Navigating social situations can be impossible without the right tools in your arsenal. That's where *Down South Paleo* is such a gift! With these recipes, Jennifer has accomplished something I could never—each recipe will bring back a flood of memories with its traditional Southern flavors and textures, without the gluten, dairy or processed junk.

As I sat with Jennifer and her family, over a meal we both cooked entirely from *Down South Paleo*, her passion and love for her craft rang loud and true. She made this book for those of us who long for the classics we loved to eat before we had to find healthier alternatives. She cooks from the heart, a place where only the best recipes are created. After trying out many of the recipes from this book, I can assure you that all of the recipes are not only fantastic, but also manage to be classic and traditional, as well as innovative in their approach to using healthier ingredients! If you want to prove to people that Paleo foods can be delicious as well as nutritious, and that no one needs to let go of their comfort food culture, then *Down South Paleo* is the cookbook you've been waiting for.

For those of you with food intolerances beyond just gluten-free, *Down South Paleo* also offers something special you won't find in most Paleo cookbooks. With each recipe marked to reflect when it is free of the top allergens, you'll know exactly if a recipe is for you at a quick glance. As someone with multiple food intolerances, including nightshades such as tomatoes and chilies, I was amazed that I was able to eat a full Mexican-inspired meal from *Down South Paleo* and still meet my dietary restrictions. Finding recipes that still deliver on flavor and texture when basic Paleo ingredients aren't involved (such as nuts, eggs and nightshades) is quite a feat that says a lot about the superb quality of these well-tested recipes!

I hope that you, too, will be reminded of loving, comforting memories with the foods you enjoy from *Down South Paleo*. I recommend curling up with a cup of Naturally Sweetened Sweet Tea and reading the entire book cover to cover. You'll find stories to warm your heart and recipes to whet your appetite, so make sure you've got pen and paper handy—you're going to want to write down a list of recipes to try!

--Stacy Toth and Matthew McCarry, bloggers at PaleoParents.com and authors of *Real Life Paleo*, *Beyond Bacon* and *Eat Like a Dinosaur*

INTRODUCTION

★ ★ ★

Howdy, y'all! I am Jennifer, founder of Predominantly Paleo, a hub for creative grain-free, dairy-free recipes made from whole foods! My goal in sharing my recipes is and has always been the same: make delicious food that anyone can enjoy, from kids to adults, including those eating a standard American diet. If you've read my blog, you know I am a Southern girl through and through with Texas roots that run as deep as the bluebonnets are plentiful. I am a fourth-generation Texan, and although I have lived all over the U.S. and abroad, my heart stays firmly planted back home.

This book, *Down South Paleo*, was written for all of you who take comfort and joy in mama's home cookin', no matter where you reside. It is filled with over 100 recipes nestled south of the Mason-Dixon line, including soul food, Tex-Mex, Cajun and creole, home cookin' and Gulf seafood-inspired dishes. What makes this different from other Southern cookbooks? All of the recipes are free of grains, dairy, refined sugars and overly processed ingredients.

Aside from my love of Southern food, this book was born from a very personal story of suffering and illness. A few years ago, my health began to rapidly decline. What began with anxiety and mild malaise soon turned into a laundry list of diagnoses. Labels like Lyme disease, nutritional deficiencies, autoimmune thyroid disease, leaky gut, adrenal fatigue and chronic fatigue syndrome quickly decorated my medical files. After extensive doctors visits, lab tests and medications, both holistic and mainstream, I shifted my approach when my condition only worsened.

I began removing foods that might be causing inflammation and started adding in nutritious foods that were missing. As I did this, I started reclaiming my life, little by little, and witnessed debilitating symptoms lift slowly over time. I realized that there might be others like me and felt driven to share both my recipes and my story.

Naturally, I've always had a soft spot for my Southern folk, their genuine smiles and inviting warmth. They also make some outrageously tempting foods like chicken-fried steak, coconut custard pie, cornbread and fried okra. While delicious, these foods tend to be laden with rancid vegetable oils, refined white sugar, conventionally raised meats, and bleached wheat flour. For those seeking a lifestyle with fewer inflammatory foods, those listed above are hard to come by, but often craved. My mission in writing *Down South Paleo* was to recreate all those Southern

favorites and many more, but with high-quality cooking fats, grain-free alternatives and natural, less-refined sweeteners. I've even reinvented Tex-Mex by replacing corn with yuca-based recipes. You'll find an entire chapter of these grain-free crispy treasures in the back of the book (page 184) and scattered throughout the chapters as well. I have poured my heart into writing these recipes so that you can experience a lil' taste of home, only better! From my home to yours, happy noshing, y'all!

WHEN THE ROOSTER CROWS

One thing is for certain: a cowboy can hardly wrangle all the live-long day without a good start in the morning. This chapter takes a bunch of Southern and Tex-Mex breakfast favorites and recreates them with only whole foods and love.

You don't have to be an early riser to appreciate a good hearty breakfast. From Lone Star Huevos Rancheros (page 16) to Paleo Pecan Waffles (page 15), this morning fare is made sans white flour. Yep, even Grandma's Grain-Free Biscuits and Sausage Gravy (page 28); you can bet the farm on it that there is no grain or dairy in sight!

PALEO PECAN WAFFLES

(GRAIN-, DAIRY-, SOY-, NIGHTSHADE-FREE)

If you've ever visited the state of Georgia, you know that pecans are one of the four major food groups. Whether you put 'em in pies or encrust fish with 'em, pecans are for lovin' and for eatin'! These waffles are made grain-free by using ground pecans as the flour and are dang tasty.

YIELD: 4 THICK WAFFLES

2 cups (300 g) pecan pieces

½ cup (60 g) tapioca flour

2 eggs

¼ cup (30 g) water chestnut flour

½ cup (120 ml) flax milk (or other dairy-free milk)

½ tsp sea salt

4 tbsp (60 ml) pure maple syrup

1 tsp (5 ml) pure vanilla extract

½ cup (120 ml) coconut oil, melted

1 tsp (3 g) baking soda

FOR SERVING

Dairy-Free Butter (page 141)

Fruit

Maple syrup

Preheat your waffle iron, and combine all of the ingredients in a blender. Blend on high until the batter is creamy, around 1 minute, and then pour into the greased waffle iron molds, being sure not to overfill. Follow your waffle iron's instructions on cooking time, typically taking around 5 minutes or so to cook through. Serve with my Dairy-Free Butter and top with fruit or additional maple syrup.

LONE STAR HUEVOS RANCHEROS

(GRAIN-, DAIRY-, NUT-, SOY-FREE)

This breakfast favorite typically situates a crispy corn tortilla under all the other tasty ingredients. This grain-free alternative offers a delicious, crispy tostada fashioned out of yuca root. Paired with the most amazing ranchero sauce, this dish will put the spurs right onto your boots!

YIELD: 6 SERVINGS

FOR THE RANCHERO SAUCE

1 onion, diced

1 tbsp (15 ml) avocado oil (or preferred cooking fat)

¼ cup (15 g) minced fresh cilantro

1 jalapeño pepper, seeded and minced

2 garlic cloves, minced

¼ tsp cayenne

8 oz (227 g) crushed tomatoes

2 cups (470 ml) organic chicken stock (or homemade)

¾ tsp cumin

Pinch salt if desired

FOR ASSEMBLING

6 Tostadas (page 188) or substitute with hearts of romaine

12 pastured eggs, sunny side up or fried

2 avocados, peeled, pitted and sliced

Fresh cilantro to taste

To make the ranchero sauce, combine the diced onion and avocado oil in a medium-size skillet. Sauté over high heat, stirring occasionally to prevent burning. Once the onions are translucent and start to brown, after about 10 minutes, add in the remaining ranchero sauce ingredients. Bring to a simmer and continue stirring until the sauce reduces by almost half, about 15–20 minutes.

To assemble the huevos rancheros, place a tostada on a plate and place 2 cooked eggs in the center of the tostada. On one side of the eggs, spoon one-sixth of the ranchero sauce, and on the other side of the eggs, place a couple of slices of avocado. Sprinkle fresh cilantro on top to taste. Repeat until all 6 servings are plated. Serve hot!

CORNED BEEF HASH WITH BROWN GRAVY

(GRAIN-, DAIRY-, NUT-, SOY-, NIGHTSHADE-FREE)

Corned beef hash has been a brunch-time favorite for generations. This Southern version incorporates sweet potatoes and brown gravy to really put some sizzle in your skillet!

YIELD: 4 SERVINGS

FOR THE CORNED BEEF HASH

1 medium onion, diced

1 large sweet potato, diced

1 cup (235 ml) organic beef bone broth (homemade when possible)

1 lb (454 g) cooked organic corned beef, chopped or shredded

FOR THE GRAVY

1 tbsp (8 g) tapioca flour

1 tbsp (15 ml) olive oil

2 tbsp (30 ml) full-fat organic coconut milk

1 cup (235 ml) organic beef bone broth (homemade when possible)

¼ tsp freshly ground black pepper

Sea salt to taste

FOR SERVING

4 sunny-side-up eggs (optional)

To make the corned beef hash, place the diced onion and sweet potato in a large, deep skillet over medium-high heat and pour the beef bone broth over the vegetables. Cover the skillet and allow the sweet potatoes to soften, around 20 minutes. Remove the lid and stir the ingredients. Now allow the vegetables to cook for another 5 minutes without the lid, stirring on occasion. Next, mix in the corned beef, stir and cook for 5 more minutes, until heated through. Turn the heat to low while you make the gravy.

To make the gravy, combine the tapioca flour and oil in a small saucepan. Turn the heat on medium and stir for about a minute. Now add in the coconut milk and continue stirring for a minute more. Next, pour in the beef bone broth and whisk until the gravy starts to thicken, approximately 5 more minutes. Once the desired consistency is achieved, remove from the heat at once and season with black pepper and sea salt if needed. Spoon over the corned beef hash while still warm. As an option you may top the hash with a sunny-side-up egg for an extra source of protein!

AUSTIN MIGAS

(GRAIN-, DAIRY-, NUT-, SOY-FREE)

This breakfast favorite will make even the most timid coyote howl. Packed with fresh vegetables, jalapeño for kick and homemade tortilla chips, it will quickly become a staple in any home!

YIELD: 4 SERVINGS

1 small red bell pepper, seeded and minced

1 jalapeño, seeded and minced

1 onion, diced

¼ cup (45 g) diced tomatoes, any variety

1 tbsp (15 ml) avocado oil, lard or preferred cooking fat

7 pastured eggs

¼ cup (60 ml) flax milk (or other dairy-free milk)

½ tsp salt

¼ tsp cracked black pepper

¼ tsp onion powder

1 cup (60 g) chopped cilantro

Tortilla Chips (page 187), broken into thin strips (can be omitted or substituted with store-bought sweet potato chips)

Sauté the red bell pepper, jalapeño, onion and diced tomatoes in the avocado oil in a large skillet over medium-high heat until they become softened and translucent, about 10 minutes.

While the vegetables are cooking, whisk together the eggs and flax milk in a bowl, until well combined. Once the veggies are cooked, add in the eggs and continue cooking over medium-high heat. Add in the remaining seasonings except for the cilantro. Scramble the eggs until cooked through, around 10 minutes, being careful not to let them burn. Right before removing from the heat, add in the cilantro and homemade tortilla chips. Cook for an additional 3 minutes and then serve.

TEXAS BLUEBONNET BIRDS' NESTS

(GRAIN-, DAIRY-, NUT-, SOY-, NIGHTSHADE-FREE)

With only a handful of ingredients, these birds' nests are satisfying and packed with flavor.
They are a crowd-pleaser for the whole family; you can bet the farm on it!

YIELD: 4 SERVINGS

1 lb (454 g) pastured breakfast sausage, uncooked

2 pastured eggs

2 tsp (2 g) minced chives

¼ tsp pepper

¼ tsp sea salt

¼ tsp garlic powder

Preheat the oven to 350°F (180°C, or gas mark 4).

In a mini muffin tin, take approximately 1 tablespoon (15 g) of the breakfast sausage and press it into a single muffin cup. Press it down and up against the sides of the cup, creating a hollow center. Repeat with the remaining sausage until you have filled 16 of the mini muffin cups.

In a mixing bowl, whisk together the eggs, chives, pepper, sea salt and garlic powder until well combined. Using a spoon, distribute the egg mixture evenly among the sausage "nests," being careful not to overfill.

Bake for 12–18 minutes, or until cooked through. Watch to prevent overcooking. Remove the muffin tin from the oven and remove the "nests" from the muffin cups. They should easily pop out of the muffin tin using a spoon.

TAQUERIA BREAKFAST BURRITO

(GRAIN-, DAIRY-, NUT-, SOY-FREE)

Why wait 'til supper to chow down on a burrito when you can start your mornin' with one?! This breakfast burrito wraps a warm, soft, grain-free tortilla around a delicious blend of eggs, tomato and diced onion.

YIELD: 4 SERVINGS

8 pastured eggs

¼ cup (60 ml) flax milk (or other dairy-free milk)

1 vine-ripened tomato, diced

¼ cup (40 g) minced red onion

¼ tsp garlic powder

¼ tsp onion powder

½ tsp sea salt

½ tsp ground black pepper

2 tsp (10 ml) olive or avocado oil

Handful of chopped cilantro, divided (optional)

4 large Tortillas (page 189)

FOR SERVING

Homemade Salsa (page 128, optional)

In a bowl, whisk together the eggs and milk. Add the tomato, onion, garlic powder, onion powder, sea salt and pepper and stir to combine.

Heat the oil in a large skillet over medium-high heat. Once hot, pour in the egg mixture, and allow it to begin to set. Once the underneath starts to cook, use a spatula to shift the eggs so the uncooked portion is given access to the heat. Repeat until the eggs are scrambled and then remove from the heat. Add the cilantro if desired.

Spoon one-fourth of the scrambled egg mixture into the center of each tortilla. Fold in the sides of the tortilla until there is just about an inch (2.5 cm) or so between them and then roll the partially folded burrito from top to bottom until it is sealed off on all sides. Feeling saucy? Top these beauties with Homemade Salsa.

FRIED EGGS BENEDICT + "CORNBREAD" WAFFLES

(GRAIN-, DAIRY-, SOY-FREE)

Although the origin of eggs Benedict might have been a little farther north, this version is no doubt Southern! The English muffin is replaced with a "cornbread" waffle, and the Canadian bacon with honey maple ham. And of course, rich, creamy, dairy-free hollandaise tops it off!

YIELD: 3 SERVINGS

FOR THE "CORNBREAD" WAFFLES

1 cup (120 g) blanched almond flour

3 tbsp (24 g) coconut flour

1 tsp (3 g) baking soda

4 pastured eggs

½ cup (120 ml) palm shortening

3 tbsp (45 ml) local raw honey

3 tbsp (45 ml) 100% pure applesauce

1 tsp (5 ml) apple cider vinegar

FOR THE FRIED EGGS

1 tbsp (15 ml) bacon fat, avocado oil or preferred cooking fat

6 pastured eggs

Sea salt and pepper to taste

FOR THE HOLLANDAISE SAUCE

4 pastured egg yolks

2 tsp (10 ml) lemon juice

2 tbsp (30 ml) organic full-fat coconut milk

4 tbsp (60 ml) light olive oil

⅛ tsp sea salt

Pinch of paprika

FOR SERVING

6 oz (168 g) pastured maple honey ham, sliced and warmed

1 ½ cups (105 g) baby spinach

To make the waffles, begin by preheating your waffle maker. Combine the flours and baking soda in one bowl and then combine the eggs, shortening, honey, applesauce and vinegar in another. Incorporate the wet ingredients into the dry, using a hand mixer if necessary to ensure the ingredients are mixed well. Once the waffle iron is hot, pour one-third of the mixture in the center and follow your waffle maker's instructions, removing the cooked waffle once prompted. Make the remaining 2 waffles and set aside.

To make the eggs, preheat the preferred cooking fat in a large skillet over medium-high heat. Crack each egg into the skillet carefully and fry on each side for about 2–3 minutes, or until the desired doneness. Add salt and pepper to taste. Set the eggs aside briefly while you make the hollandaise.

To make the hollandaise, whisk together the egg yolks and lemon juice vigorously for 2 minutes. Heat the coconut milk and olive oil in a small saucepan over high heat for about a minute, or until heated through. Slowly drizzle the hot oil mix into the egg yolks, whisking vigorously. Once the oil is completely incorporated, add the salt and paprika.

To serve, first layer a single waffle on a plate. Layer 2 ounces (56 g) of the ham and one-third of the spinach leaves on top of the waffle. Next stack 2 eggs on top of the spinach. Finally, drizzle with one-third of the hollandaise sauce. Serve right away!

CHORIZO BREAKFAST TACOS + TOMATILLO PICO DE GALLO

(GRAIN-, DAIRY-, NUT-, SOY-FREE)

Think tacos are just for supper? No way, José! This here breakfast taco packs some heat with the chorizo, then cools things off with a tomatillo pico de gallo. This is one breakfast that will leave you craving more.

YIELD: 4 SERVINGS

FOR THE TACO FILLING

8 pastured eggs

½ cup (120 ml) flax milk (or preferred dairy-free milk)

½ tsp garlic sea salt

1 tbsp (15 ml) olive oil or preferred cooking fat

1 lb (454 g) organic chorizo, casings removed

FOR THE TOMATILLO PICO DE GALLO

3 tomatillos, husked, rinsed and minced

½ red onion, minced

½ tsp garlic sea salt

Handful of cilantro, chopped

Juice from 1 lime

FOR SERVING

4 large or 8 small Tortillas (page 189) or substitute with hearts of romaine

To make the taco filling, in a mixing bowl, combine the eggs, milk and garlic sea salt. Whisk until well combined. In a large skillet over medium heat, scramble the eggs in the olive oil until light and fluffy but cooked through, about 7–8 minutes. Use a spatula to break up the eggs while cooking to prevent burning. Set the eggs aside. In a medium-size skillet, cook the chorizo over high heat, breaking it up into crumbles as it cooks. This will take about 5–7 minutes; set the chorizo aside.

To make the pico de gallo, combine all the ingredients and stir. Keep chilled until ready for use.

Premade tortillas may be warmed in the toaster oven or regular oven at 300°F (150°C, or gas mark 2) for several minutes; keeping the heat low will warm them while preventing them from crisping up like tostadas.

To assemble the breakfast tacos, into each tortilla, scoop a spoonful of eggs, followed by a spoonful or two of chorizo and finally top with pico de gallo.

COCONUT PANCAKES WITH PEACH COMPOTE

(GRAIN-, DAIRY-, NUT-, SOY-, NIGHTSHADE-FREE)

There is just somethin' about pancakes on a griddle that makes the troubles of the world melt away.
Topped with peach compote, these nut-free pancakes are the perfect comfort food.

YIELD: 3 SERVINGS

FOR THE PANCAKES

2 tbsp (30 ml) olive oil (or preferred cooking fat), plus more for griddle

½ cup (60 g) coconut flour

1 cup (235 ml) coconut milk (or other dairy-free milk)

3 eggs

½ tsp baking soda

1 tsp (5 ml) pure vanilla extract

2 tbsp (24 g) coconut palm sugar

FOR THE PEACH COMPOTE

10 oz (284 g) chopped peaches, fresh or frozen

2 tbsp (30 ml) water

2 tbsp (24 g) coconut palm sugar

½ tsp pure vanilla extract

Preheat the griddle (or skillet) over medium-low heat with enough oil to grease the bottom.

To make the pancakes, combine all the pancake ingredients in a mixing bowl and stir until well combined. Allow the batter to thicken slightly by letting it sit for a minute or two before cooking. Once the cooking surface is hot, pour silver dollar–size pancakes, a few at a time, onto your griddle (or skillet); they should be no more than 3 or 4 inches (7.5 or 10 cm) in diameter in order to ease flipping. Keeping the heat on medium-low will help prevent burning, as coconut flour has a tendency to burn. Cook for 2–3 minutes on the first side. Using a thin flexible spatula, flip the pancakes when ready and then cook for another 2 minutes on the other side. Remove them from the griddle and repeat until all the batter has been used.

To make the peach compote, combine all the ingredients in a small saucepan over high heat, stirring continuously for about 15 minutes. The liquids will reduce and produce a thick syrup and the peaches will be nicely softened. Serve the pancakes with a spoonful of compote on top.

GRANDMA'S GRAIN-FREE BISCUITS
+ SAUSAGE GRAVY

(GRAIN-, DAIRY-, EGG-, SOY-, NIGHTSHADE-FREE)

Let's be honest, shall we? Homemade biscuits and gravy are like the pot of gold at the end of the rainbow. They are the most prized Southern breakfast, and when you can make 'em right, YOU are as good as gold!

YIELD: 3 SERVINGS

FOR THE BISCUITS

1 cup (120 g) blanched almond flour

½ cup (60 g) tapioca flour

3 tbsp (24 g) water chestnut flour

½ tsp sea salt

1 tsp (3 g) baking soda

2 tbsp (30 ml) bacon fat

½ cup (120 ml) full-fat coconut milk

1 tbsp (15 ml) local raw honey

FOR THE GRAVY

1 lb (454 g) pastured breakfast sausage

1 (13.5 oz [378 g]) can full-fat organic coconut milk

¼ cup (60 ml) water

3 tbsp (24 g) tapioca flour

½ tsp sea salt

½ tsp freshly cracked black pepper

Preheat the oven to 400°F (200°C, or gas mark 6).

To make the biscuits, combine the three flours with the sea salt and baking soda in a bowl. Add the bacon fat, mashing it into the flours as you would shortening. You want to be sure to incorporate it well before adding the liquids so there are no lumps. Next, slowly pour in the coconut milk, stirring continuously. Lastly, add the honey and stir. Let the mixture sit for about 5 minutes. On a parchment-lined baking sheet, spoon about ¼ cup (60 g) of the mixture at a time. Because these do not have self-rising white flour or eggs, they will not rise much. For this reason, you'll want to shape them in a vertical dome as much as possible if you want to avoid flatter biscuits. They are delicious either way; it's more of an aesthetic preference. Bake them for about 8–10 minutes, until golden. Remove from the oven and let cool slightly.

To make the gravy, cook the sausage in a medium-size skillet over medium-high heat until no longer pink. Turn the heat to low. On another burner, heat the coconut milk and water over medium heat, reserving ¼ cup (60 ml) of the liquid to make a slurry. Add the tapioca flour to the reserved liquid and stir until the flour is well incorporated. Pour the slurry into the heated coconut milk/water mixture. Turn the heat up to medium-high and whisk the mixture until it begins to thicken. Once it reaches the desired gravy consistency, typically after about 3–5 minutes, you can pour the mixture over the sausage in the other skillet. Add the sea salt and black pepper, stir once more, and your gravy is ready to pour over your warm, homemade grain-free biscuits!

CINNAMON PECAN COFFEE CAKE

(GRAIN-, DAIRY-, SOY-, NIGHTSHADE-FREE)

If you are a believer that cake isn't just for birthdays, mark this recipe. Because we Southerners believe cake is for all occasions, including breakfast! Celebrating before 9 a.m.? Do it up y'all! This is delicious with New Orleans Café au Lait (page 176).

YIELD: 9 SERVINGS

FOR THE CAKE

1 cup (150 g) pecan halves

¼ cup (60 ml) avocado, coconut or olive oil

3 pastured eggs

½ cup (120 ml) full-fat coconut milk (or preferred dairy-free milk)

¼ cup (30 g) coconut flour

¼ cup (30 g) tapioca

¼ cup (30 g) water chestnut flour

¼ tsp sea salt

⅓ cup (65 g) coconut palm sugar

1 tsp (5 ml) pure vanilla extract

½ tsp ground cinnamon

FOR THE TOPPING

½ cup (75 g) pecan pieces

¼ tsp ground cinnamon

2 tbsp (24 g) coconut palm sugar

2 tbsp (30 ml) avocado, coconut or olive oil

Preheat the oven to 350°F (180°C, or gas mark 4).

To make the cake, combine all the ingredients in a blender. Blend until you have a creamy consistency, then pour into an 8 x 8-inch (20 x 20-cm) greased baking pan or casserole dish.

Alternatively, you can bake this in a loaf pan. Bake for 20 minutes.

To make the topping, while the cake is baking, combine the topping ingredients. Remove the coffee cake from the oven and spread the topping over the top of the cake. Return to the oven for an additional 10–15 minutes, until the topping is crisp. Remove from the oven and allow the cake to cool for 10 minutes before slicing. Serve warm.

SUPPER (AND OTHER MAIN COURSES)

If you have ever been called to "supper," then you know it is a Southern table that awaits you. Even if the meal is not Southern in nature, the word supper certainly is. In fact, as a child, I never realized the word dinner referred to the same meal, as supper was always the one used to describe the evening meal.

Southern suppers can be anything from a bowl of hearty chili to a big ol' basket of fried chicken, and from seafood to steak. The meals can be as simple as protein and veggies, but they are always satisfying and filling. In this chapter you'll find mini grain-free chicken pot pies, fried catfish with tartar sauce, chicken 'n waffles and tortilla soup, to name a few. Of course, traditionally a Southern supper includes a baked good like a biscuit or cornbread as the perfect means to sop up extra sauce! But for those, you'll have to mosey on over to the "Freshly Baked + Sweetie Pies" chapter (page 137)!

MAMA'S FRIED CHICKEN

(GRAIN-, DAIRY-, NUT-, SOY-, NIGHTSHADE-FREE)

This is everything you think of when you think of good ol' homemade fried chicken—hot, crispy, juicy, savory!
Leave out the dairy and grain for a Paleo twist on an old Southern favorite!

YIELD: 6 SERVINGS

½ cup (120 ml) full-fat coconut milk

½ cup (120 g) homemade mayonnaise
(or high-quality store-bought)

2 pastured eggs

½ cup (60 g) tapioca flour

½ cup (60 g) water chestnut flour

¼ cup (30 g) coconut flour

2 tsp (6 g) sea salt

1 tsp (3 g) freshly cracked black pepper

½ tsp onion powder

½ tsp garlic powder

Lard, avocado oil or preferred frying fat

1 whole organic chicken, cut into pieces
(breast, thigh, drumsticks, wings)

Preheat the oven to 350°F (180°C, or gas mark 4).

On a clean plate, whisk together the coconut milk, mayonnaise and eggs until combined well. (Alternatively, you may omit the egg from the milk mixture, though the crust may have a more difficult time adhering.) On another clean plate, mix together the three flours and seasonings. Coat the bottom of a large, deep skillet (cast iron works well) with about ½ inch (1.3 cm) of cooking fat and preheat over medium-high heat.

Take one piece of chicken and coat it on both sides with the milk and egg mixture, then dredge it in the seasoned flour on both sides. Shake off any excess but be sure to re-dredge any uncoated spots to create an even crust. Repeat until all the chicken is coated.

Working in small batches so as not to overcrowd the skillet, fry the chicken for approximately 4–5 minutes per side, or until each side is nicely browned. Once all the chicken pieces have been fried, lay them on a wire baking rack set on top of a baking pan and bake for another 20 minutes, or until the chicken is cooked through. Remove from the oven and serve right away.

BLUEBERRY BRISKET

(GRAIN-, DAIRY-, NUT-, EGG-, SOY-, NIGHTSHADE-FREE)

Don't have a giant mesquite-filled smoker to prepare your brisket? No problem! This tender brisket is made right on your stove top and will literally melt in your mouth!

YIELD: 4 SERVINGS

¼ cup (60 ml) olive oil (or preferred cooking fat)

1 tsp (3 g) freshly ground black pepper

½ tsp sea salt

1 brisket, grass-fed if possible (about 4 lbs [1816 g])

1 large onion, thinly sliced

4 cups (940 ml) organic beef broth, homemade if possible

5 cloves garlic, minced

6 large carrots, coarsely chopped

1 cup (150 g) blueberries

FOR SERVING

Mixed greens

Heat the oil in a large stockpot over medium-high heat. Rub the ground pepper and sea salt on both sides of the brisket and brown in the oil for about 7 minutes, then flip the brisket over to brown the other side. Once both sides of brisket are nicely browned, place the sliced onion in the bottom of the stockpot, underneath the brisket. Place the brisket back on top of the onion. Pour the beef broth over the brisket and add the garlic, carrots and blueberries. Bring to a simmer, cover and continue simmering for about 4 hours. Remove the brisket from the pot, slice and serve with the vegetables and juices and whatever greens you wish.

MINI CHICKEN POT PIES

(GRAIN-, DAIRY-, SOY-, NIGHTSHADE-FREE)

Chicken pot pies are the ultimate comfort food and a sure way to know you're loved. Make these lil' personal-size ones so there are no squabbles over the delicious crust!

YIELD: 4 SERVINGS

FOR THE FILLING

1 lb (454 g) organic chicken breasts

3 tbsp (45 ml) lard, bacon drippings or preferred cooking fat

3 tbsp (24 g) arrowroot flour, more as needed

4 cups (940 ml) organic chicken broth

3 large organic carrots, chopped

1 organic yellow onion, chopped

1 cup (150 g) organic peas

1 tsp (3 g) pepper

1 tsp (3 g) garlic salt

½ tsp onion powder

2 bay leaves

FOR THE CRUST

2 cups (240 g) almond flour

½ cup (60 g) arrowroot flour

1 egg, beaten

½ tsp sea salt

3 tbsp (45 ml) palm shortening, melted, more as needed

Preheat the oven to 375°F (190°C, or gas mark 5).

To make the filling, poach the chicken breasts in a pot of simmering water for 15 minutes, or until cooked through. Chop or shred the chicken and set aside.

In a skillet over medium heat, whisk together the lard and arrowroot flour until well combined. Add the chicken broth and then the chopped carrots, onion, peas and seasonings to the broth mixture. Bring to a simmer for 10 minutes, until it begins to thicken. If it does not seem to thicken enough, add more arrowroot flour (making a slurry first), stir and continue to simmer until thickened to the desired consistency. Remove from the heat, remove and discard the bay leaves, add the diced chicken, combine well and set aside.

To make the crust, combine the almond flour, arrowroot flour, egg, sea salt and melted palm shortening. If the crust is too crumbly, add more melted shortening, a teaspoon (5 ml) at a time. Fill individual oven-safe bowls or mini pie tins with the filling three-fourths of the way full. Take a handful of the dough and roll into a ball, flatten and place over the mixture in the bowl; repeat for all the bowls.

Place the bowls on a baking sheet and bake for 15–20 minutes, watching to prevent burning, until golden and bubbly. Serve hot.

KING RANCH CASSEROLE

(GRAIN-, DAIRY-, SOY-FREE)

Traditionally made with corn tortillas, a truckload of cheese and a can of cream of mushroom soup (you know the one), this comfort food is hardly health food. My revamp still layers in all the taste and delivers a little piece of mama's cookin'.

YIELD: 8 SERVINGS

FOR THE TORTILLA LAYER (MAY BE OMITTED TO MAKE CASSEROLE WITH FILLING AND TOPPING ONLY)

2 cups (360 g) peeled and chopped yuca root

1 ripe plantain, peeled

3 tbsp (45 ml) avocado oil (or preferred cooking fat)

½ tsp sea salt

½ cup (60 g) finely ground water chestnut flour

FOR THE SAUCE

8 oz (227 g) button mushrooms, diced

1 large yellow onion, diced

1 red bell pepper, seeded and diced

2 tsp (10 ml) avocado oil (or preferred cooking fat)

3 cloves garlic, minced

1 (10 oz [280 g]) can organic diced tomatoes and green chiles, drained

4 cups (940 ml) organic chicken stock

½ tsp paprika

½ tsp cumin

¾ tsp chili powder

½ tsp onion powder

¼ tsp freshly cracked black pepper

½ cup (120 ml) full-fat coconut milk

6 tbsp (48 g) water chestnut flour

FOR THE "CHEESE" TOPPING

1 cup (150 g) cashews, soaked for 3–4 hours and drained

3 tbsp (45 ml) water

½ tsp dried parsley

¼ tsp apple cider vinegar

¼ tsp onion powder

¼ tsp sea salt

1 egg

1 lb (454 g) shredded chicken breast

Chopped fresh cilantro, for garnish (optional)

To make the tortilla layers, bring a medium-size stockpot filled halfway with water to a boil over high heat, add the peeled yuca root and cook for 25 minutes, or until fork-tender. Drain the water and remove the fibrous core from the center of the yuca once cool enough to handle.

Using a high-powered blender, combine the yuca, plantain, oil and salt until a dough forms. If you have a blender with a tamper, using the tamper vigorously will help pull the yuca chunks into the blades. Spoon the dough onto a piece of parchment paper and allow it to cool for about 5 minutes.

While the dough is cooling, preheat the oven to 350°F (180°C, or gas mark 4).

Add the water chestnut flour to the yuca dough, using your hands to incorporate it well. Place another piece of parchment paper on top of the dough and, using a rolling pin, roll it out until the dough is about ⅓ inch (8 mm) thick. Make a large rectangle with your dough instead of round tortillas, as this will layer nicely in your casserole dish. Transfer the bottom piece of parchment paper and the dough to a large baking sheet and bake for 25 minutes.

To make the sauce, in a deep skillet, sauté the diced mushrooms, onion and red bell pepper in the oil over medium-high heat for about 10 minutes. Once the vegetables are tender, add in the garlic, diced tomatoes, green chiles and chicken stock. Bring the mixture to a simmer and add the paprika, cumin, chili powder, onion powder and black pepper. Allow the mixture to simmer for about 10 minutes while the vegetables continue to cook. In a separate bowl, combine the coconut milk and water chestnut flour until well combined, then add the mixture to the skillet. Continue to simmer until the sauce thickens, about 5 more minutes.

To make the cheese topping, blend the soaked cashews, water, parsley, apple cider vinegar, onion powder, sea salt and egg in a blender or food processor. Blend until creamy. Set aside.

Now you can begin layering your casserole. If you prefer a thicker casserole, you can use a smaller casserole dish, such as a 9 x 9-inch (23 x 23-cm). Otherwise, a standard 9 x 13-inch (23 x 33-cm) will yield a thinner, larger casserole. Take the tortilla layer, which has been baked through, and cut it according to your pan selection. You will need 2 pieces total for layering. After sizing accordingly, take one piece of the tortilla and place it in the bottom of the casserole dish. Take one-third of the sauce mixture and spread it evenly over the tortilla layer. Now spoon half of the shredded chicken on top of the sauce. Next, place another tortilla layer on top of the chicken, and spoon another third of sauce on top of the tortilla. Spread the remaining chicken on top of the sauce and then make one last layer of sauce. Finally, top with remaining cheese mixture and spread evenly. Bake for 25 minutes, until cooked through and bubbly. Serve piping hot, garnished with fresh cilantro if desired.

HOME-STYLE CHICKEN-FRIED STEAK + CREAM GRAVY

(GRAIN-, NUT-, DAIRY-, SOY-, NIGHTSHADE-FREE)

Everyone knows if you take a trip down South that you will not return home without witnessing
a big giant chicken-fried steak platter the size of your head. Topped with cream gravy, it's as Southern as it gets.
You'll be sayin' "y'all" like the locals before long!

YIELD: 4 STEAKS

FOR THE STEAKS

¼ cup (30 g) coconut flour

¼ cup (30 g) finely ground water chestnut flour

¼ cup (30 g) arrowroot flour

¼ tsp onion powder

¼ tsp garlic powder

¾ tsp sea salt

½ tsp cracked black pepper

Paprika to taste

⅓ cup (80 ml) full-fat organic coconut milk

1 egg

Lard, avocado oil or preferred cooking fat for frying

4 cubed steaks (1 lb [454 g] total), organic grass-fed preferred

FOR THE CREAM GRAVY

1 cup (235 ml) flax milk (or preferred dairy-free milk)

2 tbsp (16 g) arrowroot flour

¼ tsp sea salt or more to taste

¼ tsp black pepper or more to taste

¼ tsp onion powder

To make the steaks, combine the three flours, onion powder, garlic powder, sea salt, black pepper and paprika on a clean plate. In a wide, shallow bowl, whisk together the coconut milk and egg to make an egg wash. This will help the crust adhere nicely to the meat.

Heat the cooking fat in a medium-size skillet over medium-high heat. You'll want to generously coat the bottom of the pan.

One at a time, coat each cubed steak in the egg wash on both sides, then dredge in the flour on each side until well coated. Fry one or two coated cubed steaks at a time until browned on each side. By using a thin flexible spatula, you can help prevent the crust from breaking off as you flip them. Once nicely browned and cooked throughout, remove from the heat and repeat as necessary until all the steaks are cooked.

To make the gravy, combine all the ingredients in a pan over medium-high heat and whisk continually until the gravy starts to thicken. Remove from the heat at once before the gravy congeals too much. Serve hot with the steaks.

MISSISSIPPI FRIED CATFISH + HOMEMADE TARTAR SAUCE

(GRAIN-, DAIRY-, SOY-FREE)

Traditionally breaded in cornmeal and deep-fried, standard Southern catfish recipes are far from Paleo. Luckily, this one creates that same crunchy taste and pairs it with homemade tartar sauce, far better than you'll find dining out!

YIELD: 4 SERVINGS

FOR THE HOMEMADE TARTAR SAUCE

½ cup (120 g) homemade mayonnaise (or high-quality store-bought)

4 tsp (20 g) dill relish

1 tsp (3 g) onion powder

½ tsp minced garlic

1 tbsp (15 ml) lemon juice

FOR THE FISH

Lard (or preferred cooking fat), for frying

⅓ cup (80 ml) full-fat coconut milk

1 tbsp (15 ml) hot sauce

⅓ cup (40 g) almond meal

⅓ cup (40 g) finely ground water chestnut flour

1 tsp (3 g) Cajun seasoning

½ tsp pepper

½ tsp sea salt

4 catfish fillets (approximately 12 oz [340 g] total)

To make the tartar sauce so that it will be ready when your fish is hot and fresh coming out of the pan, mix all of the tartar sauce ingredients in a bowl with a spoon. You may refrigerate it if you want to make it in advance.

To make the fish, heat the oil over high heat in a large, deep skillet; you'll want enough oil to cover the bottom of the skillet, but it does not need to be deep enough for submersion. On a clean plate, whisk together the coconut milk and hot sauce. On another clean plate, mix together the almond meal, water chestnut flour and seasonings. Take one fillet at a time and coat with the milk mixture. Then dredge the fillet in the breading mixture, carefully coating both sides. Repeat with all remaining fillets and fry them in small batches for approximately 3–5 minutes on each side, or until cooked through. Remove from pan and place on a towel-lined plate to absorb the excess oil.

CHEF'S TIP: Using a flexible spatula will aid in flipping the fish fillets over, as they can be very delicate once cooked.

SWEET + SAVORY
SLOW COOKER PULLED PORK

(GRAIN-, DAIRY-, NUT-, EGG-, SOY-FREE)

By the taste of this, you'd think lots of effort from a skilled hand had to be behind the recipe.
But the truth is the slow cooker holds the secret to this perfectly "shreddable" sweet and savory pork.
Wonderful served alone or as a lil' "sammich."

YIELD: 5 SERVINGS

1 ½ lbs (680 grams) pork loin (or shoulder)

1 onion, sliced into rings

1 tsp (3 g) sea salt

1 tsp (3 g) paprika

¼ tsp cumin

1 tsp (3 g) garlic powder

1 tsp (1 g) dried parsley

½ tsp mustard powder

¼ cup (50 g) coconut palm sugar

2 tbsp (30 ml) apple cider vinegar

¼ cup (60 ml) local raw honey

FOR SERVING

Sweet Potato Slider Buns (page 146)

Place the pork loin in the bottom of the slow cooker. Place the onion rings around the pork. Sprinkle all the seasonings on top of the pork, saving the apple cider vinegar and honey for last. Once the pork has been seasoned, pour the vinegar on top of the pork and then drizzle the honey over the seasonings. Cook on high for about 4 hours, or until the meat shreds easily with a fork and knife. Serve on the Sweet Potato Slider Buns for a house full of smiles!

GULF COAST FRIED SHRIMP + REMOULADE SAUCE

(GRAIN-, DAIRY-, EGG-, NUT-, SOY-FREE)

If you've ever been to any of the states bordering the Gulf of Mexico, you know that fried shrimp are taken pretty darn seriously down there. Hot out of the fryer, dunked in tartar or remoulade sauce, they will almost melt in your mouth. This version uses water chestnut flour, which makes for a perfect flaky crust you'll love!

YIELD: 4 SERVINGS

FOR THE SHRIMP

Avocado oil (or preferred cooking fat), for frying

⅔ cup (160 ml) full-fat coconut milk (or other dairy-free milk)

1 ⅓ cups (160 g) finely ground water chestnut flour

⅔ cup (80 g) tapioca starch

1 tsp (3 g) sea salt

½ tsp paprika

2 tsp (6 g) garlic powder

2 tsp (6 g) onion powder

1 lb (454 g) raw, peeled tail-off shrimp

FOR THE REMOULADE

½ cup (120 g) homemade mayonnaise (or high-quality store-bought)

2 tbsp (30 g) creole mustard

1 clove garlic, minced

1 tsp (5 ml) dill pickle juice

1 tsp (3 g) paprika

⅛ tsp sea salt

To make the shrimp, heat enough avocado oil to cover the bottom of a large deep skillet or wok and place over high heat. While the oil is heating, pour the coconut milk into a clean bowl. In another clean bowl, mix the water chestnut flour, tapioca starch and all the seasonings. Take several shrimp at a time and submerge them in the coconut milk. Then transfer the shrimp to the flour bowl and dredge them until they are covered in flour. Repeat with the remaining shrimp. Place the coated shrimp in the hot oil and fry until cooked through and crispy, about 3 minutes on each side. Using a slotted spoon, remove the fried shrimp from the hot oil and place on a towel-lined plate. Repeat until all shrimp the are fried.

To make the remoulade, combine all the ingredients and serve right away with the shrimp or refrigerate for later.

CARAMELIZED ONION TURKEY MEATLOAF

(GRAIN-, DAIRY-, NUT-, SOY-FREE)

Home cooking rule #76: the way to a Southerner's heart is through a mouthwatering meatloaf recipe!
Instead of breadcrumbs and ketchup, this one uses organic diced tomatoes and coconut flour!

YIELD: 6 SERVINGS

FOR THE MEATLOAF

1 onion, diced

1 tbsp (15 ml) avocado or olive oil

⅓ cup (50 g) petite diced tomatoes

1 tsp (3 g) sea salt

1 tsp (3 g) garlic powder

1 tsp (3 g) onion powder

½ tsp pepper

2 tbsp (24 g) coconut palm sugar

1 tbsp (15 ml) high-quality
Worcestershire sauce

2 lbs (908 g) ground organic,
pastured turkey

1 pastured egg

2 tbsp (16 g) coconut flour

⅓ cup (80 ml) full-fat coconut milk

FOR THE SAUCE

⅓ cup (50 g) petite diced tomatoes

3 tbsp (36 g) maple sugar

2 tbsp (30 ml) apple cider vinegar

Preheat the oven to 350°F (180°C, or gas mark 4).

To make the meatloaf, in a small skillet, sauté the diced onion in the oil for about 12–15 minutes over medium-high heat until nicely browned. Stir occasionally to prevent burning and to promote even cooking. Once done, remove the onions from the heat and set aside. In a large bowl, add the remaining ingredients for the meatloaf and mix well by hand until all the ingredients are combined. Save the onions for mixing in last as they are still hot to the touch and can also prematurely cook the egg. Once all the ingredients are incorporated, transfer the contents to a greased loaf pan. Form the mixture into a loaf so the meat does not crumble while cooking.

To make the sauce, puree all the sauce ingredients and pour over the uncooked meatloaf. Bake for 40–50 minutes, or until cooked through. Slice and serve!

SLOW COOKER ROTISSERIE CHICKEN

(GRAIN-, DAIRY-, NUT-, EGG-, SOY-FREE)

Easy doesn't even begin to describe the simplicity of this recipe. In fact, I think even the smallest cowboy could toss this tasty, fall-off-the-bone "rotisserie" chicken together. Perfect for any day of the year!

YIELD: 4 SERVINGS

1 cup (120 g) chopped carrot

1 onion, sliced into rings

1 pastured whole chicken (3–5 lbs [1362–2270 g])

1 tsp (3 g) sea salt

1 tsp (3 g) paprika

1 tsp (1 g) dried parsley

½ tsp dried mustard

½ tsp black pepper

1 tsp (3 g) garlic powder

1 tsp (3 g) onion powder

½ tsp dried thyme

In the bottom of a large slow cooker, arrange the carrots and onion. Then set the whole chicken on top of the vegetables. Sprinkle all of the seasonings on top of the chicken, turn the slow cooker on high and cook for 4–6 hours, or until the chicken is cooked thoroughly and the meat falls off the bone. Believe it or not, additional liquids are not necessary to make this bird fork tender.

GRINGO'S SLOW COOKER TORTILLA SOUP

(GRAIN-, DAIRY-, EGG-, NUT-, SOY-FREE)

Simple yet savory, this tortilla soup is perfect for warming the soul and spicing up taste buds!
I find it just as great for entertaining as I do for serving on a low-key weeknight. If you have time,
be sure to make the Tortilla Chips (page 187) to accompany.

YIELD: 4 SERVINGS

1 lb (454 g) chicken breasts
(organic/pastured when possible)

4 cups (940 ml) chicken broth

¼ cup (60 g) organic tomato sauce

1 small bell pepper, seeded and diced

1 onion, diced

¼ cup (45 g) diced tomatoes

2 cloves garlic

1 jalapeño pepper, seeded and minced

½ tsp sea salt

½ tsp ground black pepper

¼ tsp cumin

¼ tsp chili powder

½ tsp onion powder

1 bay leaf

Juice from 1 lime

FOR SERVING

Handful of cilantro

Tortilla Chips (page 187, optional)

Dairy-free sour cream (optional)

Place the chicken breasts on the bottom of your slow cooker. Pour the chicken broth over the chicken and then add the remaining ingredients except for the garnishes. Turn the slow cooker on low and cook for around 6 hours, or cook on high for around 4 hours. Remove the bay leaf after cooking. Once the chicken is cooked through, shred it with two forks while keeping it in the soup; it should fall apart easily. Now it is ready to serve, garnished with extra cilantro, tortilla chips and dairy-free sour cream if desired.

SOUTHERN FRIED CHICKEN AND WAFFLES

(GRAIN-, DAIRY-, SOY-, NIGHTSHADE-FREE)

If ever there was a perfect pairing, this is it: sweet, savory, juicy and crunchy.
Drizzled with a little maple syrup, this one puts the "soul" in soul food!

YIELD: 4 SERVINGS

FOR THE WAFFLES

2 cups (300 g) pecan pieces

½ cup (60 g) tapioca flour

2 eggs

¼ cup (30 g) finely ground water chestnut flour

½ cup (120 ml) flax milk (or other dairy-free milk)

½ tsp sea salt

4 tbsp (60 ml) pure maple syrup

1 tsp (5 ml) pure vanilla extract

½ cup (120 ml) coconut oil, melted

1 tsp (3 g) baking soda

FOR THE CHICKEN STRIPS

1 egg

¼ cup (60 ml) full-fat coconut milk (or other dairy-free milk)

⅓ cup (40 g) arrowroot or tapioca flour

⅓ cup (40 g) water chestnut flour

3 tbsp (24 g) coconut flour

1 tsp (3 g) sea salt

½ tsp onion powder

½ tsp garlic powder

¼ tsp paprika

Lard (or preferred cooking fat), for frying

1 lb (454 g) organic chicken tenderloins

FOR SERVING

Maple syrup

Local honey

To make the waffles, preheat your waffle iron, then combine all of the waffle ingredients in a blender. Blend on high until the batter is creamy, around 1 minute, and then pour into the greased waffle iron molds, being sure not to overfill. Follow your waffle iron's instructions on cooking time; it typically takes around 5 minutes or so to cook through. Make 4 waffles.

To make the chicken strips, combine the egg and milk in a bowl and whisk together until well combined. On a clean plate, combine the arrowroot flour, water chestnut flour, coconut flour, sea salt, onion powder, garlic powder and paprika and stir together until the seasonings and flours are blended well.

Heat cooking fat in a large skillet over medium-high heat for a few minutes while you coat your chicken tenderloins. You will not be deep-frying, so add just need enough fat to coat the bottom of the skillet. Take one chicken tenderloin and dip it in the egg wash on both sides. Then dredge it in the flour mixture on both sides and shake off any extra. If you come up with "bald" spots where the flour didn't stick, dredge again until it does. Place each coated chicken tenderloin in the hot oil and fry on each side until crispy and cooked through, approximately 3–4 minutes on each side. Carefully remove the cooked chicken from the skillet and place on a towel-lined plate to absorb any excess oil. Repeat with the remaining tenderloins until they are all cooked.

To serve, stack one-fourth of the chicken strips on top of each waffle. Drizzle with real maple syrup or local honey for a touch of sweetness.

TEXAS SLOW COOKER BEEF CHILI

(GRAIN-, DAIRY-, EGG-, NUT-, SOY-FREE)

If there is one thing the Southern states take as seriously as college football season, it's the chili served during those pigskin months! This legume-free alternative packs in extra organic vegetables so you can kiss those beans adios!

YIELD: 6 SERVINGS

1 lb (454 g) grass-fed organic beef

1 green bell pepper, seeded and diced

1 large onion, diced

4 large carrots, chopped small

26 oz (728 g) finely chopped tomatoes

½ tsp ground black pepper

1 tsp (3 g) sea salt

1 tsp (3 g) onion powder

1 tbsp (4 g) chopped fresh parsley

1 tbsp (15 ml) Worcestershire sauce

4 tsp (12 g) chili powder

1 tsp (3 g) paprika

1 tsp (3 g) garlic powder

Pinch of cumin

FOR SERVING

Dairy-free sour cream (optional)

Diced onions (optional)

Sliced jalapeños (optional)

Place the ground beef in a medium-size skillet over high heat and brown, stirring, until no longer pink. Spoon it into your slow cooker, including the fat. Now place the green bell pepper, onion, carrots and tomatoes into the slow cooker. Stir all the ingredients well, then add the remaining spices and seasonings. Stir once more, cover and cook on low for 8 hours or on high for 5 hours. Top with dairy-free sour cream if desired, additional diced onions or jalapeños.

BUTTERNUT SQUASH + APPLE BISQUE

(GRAIN-, DAIRY-, EGG-, NUT-, SOY-, NIGHTSHADE-FREE)

Growing up, this bisque was a favorite for Thanksgiving in my family. To this day when the leaves start to turn, butternut squash soup in one form or another is bound to show up. This one has a hint of sweet thanks to the Granny Smith apple and a smidge of coconut sugar.

YIELD: 6 SERVINGS

1 large onion, diced

20 oz (567 g) butternut squash, coarsely chopped

1 Granny Smith apple, cored and coarsely chopped

2 large carrots, coarsely chopped

1 tbsp (15 ml) avocado oil (or preferred cooking fat)

3 cloves garlic, minced

1 tsp (3 g) sea salt

½ tsp ground white pepper

2 tbsp (24 g) coconut palm sugar

½ tsp onion powder

32 oz (908 g) free-range turkey bone broth (chicken or beef may be substituted)

FOR SERVING

Toasted pumpkin seeds (optional)

Full-fat coconut milk (optional)

In a deep stockpot over high heat, sauté the onion, squash, apple and carrots in the avocado oil for about 20 minutes, stirring occasionally. The vegetables will begin to soften and some will start to brown slightly. Now add in all the remaining seasonings and broth and bring to a boil for 35 minutes. After 35 minutes, turn the heat to low and blend in batches until the entire stockpot is pureed. A large blender works best but you can also use a handheld immersion blender, though the consistency might be less bisque-like and more soup-like. Once pureed, garnish with the toasted pumpkin seeds and a drizzle of coconut milk, if desired.

MUSTARD MAPLE CHICKEN BREAST

(GRAIN-, DAIRY-, EGG-, NUT-, SOY-, NIGHTSHADE-FREE)

Satisfy all Southern palates with this sweet and savory combo. Guaranteed to put a lil' pep in your step.

YIELD: 6 SERVINGS

2 tbsp (30 ml) olive oil (or preferred cooking fat)

2 lbs (908 g) pastured, organic boneless chicken breasts

Salt and pepper to taste

½ onion, diced

2 tbsp (30 g) stone-ground mustard

½ cup (120 ml) pure maple syrup

1 cup (235 ml) organic chicken broth (homemade when possible)

2 tsp (6 g) garlic sea salt

2 tbsp (30 ml) apple cider vinegar

½ tsp white pepper

Heat the oil over medium-high heat in a deep skillet. Next, pound the chicken breasts with a meat mallet until they are about an inch (2.5 cm) thick or so. Season the chicken with salt and pepper on both sides. Now gently place the chicken in the hot oil and cook on each side for about 3–5 minutes. If need be, cook the chicken in smaller batches so as not to overcrowd the skillet. Remove the chicken from the skillet and set aside.

Add the diced onion, mustard, syrup, broth, garlic sea salt, apple cider vinegar and white pepper to the same skillet. Allow to simmer over high heat for 5–8 minutes, or until it begins to reduce and thicken. Once it has cooked down, add the chicken breasts back in and continue cooking over high heat until the chicken is cooked all the way through and the sauce is the desired thickness. Remove from the heat and serve right away.

HILL COUNTRY BBQ MEATBALLS

(GRAIN-, DAIRY-, EGG-, NUT-FREE)

Need to get a little giddy-up back into dinner? These BBQ meatballs are guaranteed to do the trick. With sautéed onions and homemade BBQ sauce baked on top, this dish might become a new Southern favorite!

YIELD: 4 SERVINGS

FOR THE MEATBALLS

1 large onion, diced

1 tbsp (15 ml) olive oil (or preferred cooking fat)

2 lbs (908 g) grass-fed ground beef

3 cloves garlic, minced

1 tsp (3 g) ground black pepper

1 tsp (3 g) sea salt

¼ cup (60 ml) flax milk (or other dairy-free milk)

½ cup (60 g) tapioca starch

½ tsp chili powder

FOR THE BBQ SAUCE

1 cup (240 g) homemade ketchup (or high-quality store-bought)

1 cup (230 g) crushed tomatoes

½ cup (120 ml) honey

1 tsp (3 g) onion powder

1 tsp (3 g) ground black pepper

¾ tsp garlic powder

2 tsp (10 ml) liquid smoke

FOR SERVING

Mashed "Taters" (page 101)

Preheat the oven to 350°F (180°C, or gas mark 4).

To make the meatballs, in a small skillet, sauté the diced onion in the oil over medium-high heat for 8–10 minutes. Remove from the pan and let cool. Combine all the remaining meatball ingredients in a large mixing bowl and mix well with your hands, adding the sautéed onion last so it has an opportunity to cool slightly. Once all ingredients are incorporated and well combined, make the meatballs by hand, each about 2 inches (5 cm) in diameter. Place on a foil-lined baking sheet and bake for about 10 minutes.

To make the sauce, while the meatballs are baking, combine all the BBQ sauce ingredients in a blender and blend on low until pureed.

Remove the meatballs from the oven after 10 minutes, carefully transfer them to a casserole dish and spoon the BBQ sauce evenly over the tops. Bake for another 10–15 minutes, or until the meatballs are cooked through. Serve on top of Mashed "Taters" for a complete feast!

JALAPEÑO GRILLED SHRIMP

(GRAIN-, DAIRY-, NUT-, EGG-FREE)

Zesty, tangy and slightly sweet, these skewered shrimp are perfect as a stand-alone, tossed into a salad or folded up in a delicious grain-free Tortilla (page 189).

YIELD: 4 SERVINGS

1 tsp (3 g) sea salt

1 tbsp (15 ml) pure maple syrup

1 jalapeño pepper, seeded and minced

4 cloves garlic, minced

Juice of 1 clementine (or orange)

Juice of 3 limes

¼ cup (60 ml) avocado oil or olive oil

Handful of chopped cilantro

1 lb (454 g) peeled, deveined wild-caught shrimp

Combine the salt, maple syrup, jalapeño, garlic, clementine juice, lime juice, oil and cilantro in a medium-size mixing bowl, then add the shrimp, make sure they are submerged and cover with plastic wrap. Allow the shrimp to marinate for 2 hours in the fridge. If a spicier jalapeño flavor is desired, the seeds can be included in the marinade.

Preheat a gas or charcoal grill to medium-high heat.

Remove the shrimp from the marinade and run the skewers through the shrimp, stacking as many as will comfortably fit on each skewer without overcrowding. Grill the shrimp skewers for about 3 minutes on each side, or until they turn pink and are cooked through. You may choose to char them slightly, based on preference.

DOWN HOME CHICKEN + DUMPLINGS

(GRAIN-, DAIRY-, EGG-, NUT-, SOY-, NIGHTSHADE-FREE)

It's a family favorite and notoriously Southern! Typically, however, the dumplings are made with bleached flour and are off-limits to grain-free eaters. This version uses yuca to make a delicious dumpling that you won't regret eating later!

YIELD: 5 SERVINGS

FOR THE BASE

1 lb (454 g) boneless organic pastured chicken breasts

3 large carrots, chopped

3 cups (705 ml) organic chicken broth (homemade when possible)

1 onion, diced

1 dried bay leaf

½ tsp onion powder

½ tsp garlic powder

½ tsp cracked black pepper

1 tsp (3 g) poultry seasoning

1 cup (235 ml) flax milk (or other dairy-free milk)

1 tbsp (8 g) arrowroot flour

FOR THE DUMPLINGS

2 cups (360 g) peeled and coarsely chopped yuca

¼ cup (60 ml) avocado oil (or preferred cooking fat)

½ tsp garlic sea salt

3 tbsp (24 g) coconut flour

To make the base, place the chicken, carrots, broth, onion, bay leaf, onion powder, garlic powder, black pepper and poultry seasoning in a slow cooker. Turn the slow cooker on high and cook for 4–5 hours, until the chicken is cooked through. In the meantime, you may prepare the dumplings and refrigerate them. Alternatively you can prepare them closer to the end of the chicken cook time if you prefer.

To make the dumplings, fill a stockpot with water and bring to a boil over high heat. Add the yuca and boil for 20–25 minutes, until fork-tender. Drain the water and remove the yuca from the pot. Remove the woody core once the yuca is cool enough to handle.

Meanwhile, preheat the oven to 325°F (170°C, or gas mark 3) while it boils.

In a heavy-duty blender, combine the yuca, avocado oil and garlic sea salt. Blend until a dough forms, then spoon it onto a piece of parchment paper or a nonstick surface. Work in the coconut flour by hand, 1 tablespoon (8 g) at a time. Knead it like a bread dough until the flour is completely incorporated. Pinch off 1 tablespoon (15 g) of the dough at a time, roll it into a ball and then flatten it slightly. Place the raw dumplings on a parchment-lined baking sheet and bake for about 20 minutes. Carefully pull out the baking sheet and flip the dumplings over, then bake on the other side for about 20 more minutes. Once done, remove from the oven and set aside.

About 30 minutes before the chicken is done, add the flax milk and stir to combine. At this point you may also use two forks to shred the chicken, while continuing to keep it in the slow cooker. Make a slurry by taking about ¼ cup (60 ml) of the hot broth out of the slow cooker and adding the arrowroot flour, stirring until it dissolves completely. Add the slurry to the chicken and broth. Stir once more until it starts to thicken. Turn the heat down to low and drop in the baked dumplings. Serve within 10–15 minutes from the time you drop the dumplings into the mixture. These are different than flour-based dumplings and can break down if left in hot liquid for too long.

JUST LIKE MOM'S CHICKEN SPAGHETTI

(GRAIN-, DAIRY-, EGG-, NUT-, SOY-FREE)

This homegrown comfort food typically packs in refined white pasta, canned cream of mushroom soup and lots of dairy. This grain- and dairy-free version uses fresh organic veggies and sweet potatoes as noodles for a flavorful and healthy alternative to the overprocessed original!

YIELD: 6 SERVINGS

1 red bell pepper, seeded and diced

1 green bell pepper, seeded and diced

8 oz (227 g) button mushrooms, diced

1 large Vidalia onion, diced

1 tbsp (15 ml) avocado oil (or preferred cooking fat)

2 cloves garlic, minced

1 tsp (3 g) sea salt

½ tsp onion powder

½ tsp paprika

½ tsp cayenne

½ tsp cracked black pepper

2 cups (470 ml) organic beef stock (homemade when possible), divided

¼ cup (30 g) tapioca flour

1 lb (454 g) cooked organic chicken, shredded

2 sweet potatoes, spiral cut or julienned

Preheat the oven to 350°F (180°C, or gas mark 4).

In a large skillet, sauté the red bell pepper, green bell pepper, mushrooms and onion in the oil over medium heat for about 10 minutes, or until the vegetables are soft. Add the garlic, seasonings and 1 ½ cups (355 ml) of the beef stock to the skillet. Bring the mixture to a simmer. Add the tapioca flour to the remaining ½ cup (120 ml) beef stock, stirring to make a slurry. Add the slurry to the sauce and continue simmering until it begins to thicken, around 5 minutes. Add the shredded chicken and cook until the sauce is thickened and coats the chicken, then remove from the heat.

In a medium-size skillet, heat the sweet potato "noodles" until they are soft and a lot of the moisture has evaporated, about 10 minutes, then remove from the heat.

In a casserole dish, layer half the sweet potato noodles, followed by half the sauce and chicken. Make another layer with the remaining sweet potato noodles and finally top with the remaining sauce and chicken mixture. Bake for about 30 minutes, until bubbly, and serve piping hot!

SAVORY SLOW COOKER PORK CHOPS

(GRAIN-, DAIRY-, EGG-, NUT-, SOY-, NIGHTSHADE-FREE)

In the Deep South, one thing is for certain: the summer sizzles as much as the cooking! That's when our trusty slow cookers sure come in handy, to keep our food hot and our kitchens cool. These pork chops are tender and juicy and let you sip on sweet tea instead of workin' over a hot stove!

YIELD: 4 SERVINGS

1 large Vidalia onion, sliced

⅓ cup (40 g) arrowroot flour

¾ tsp sea salt

½ tsp ground black pepper

¼ tsp onion powder

½ tsp garlic powder

½ tsp dried parsley

4 pork chops (pastured when possible)

3 cups (705 ml) beef broth

1 bay leaf

Line your slow cooker with the sliced onion. Then on a clean plate, combine the arrowroot flour, salt, pepper, onion powder, garlic powder and parsley. Dredge the pork chops in the seasoned flour, then lay them on top of the sliced onions in your slow cooker. If you have remaining flour, which is likely, sprinkle the rest on top of your coated pork chops. This will help thicken the gravy as the pork chops cook. Pour the beef broth over the pork chops and drop the bay leaf into the broth. Cook on high for 4 hours or low for about 6 hours.

Once they are fork-tender, remove the pork chops from the slow cooker. If your gravy is not at the desired consistency, make a slurry by combining 1 tablespoon (8 g) arrowroot flour with a small amount of gravy. Combine well, then pour the slurry into the slow cooker and stir until thickened. If desired, in a medium-size skillet, you may quickly brown the pork chops on both sides over medium heat after slow cooking is complete. Otherwise, serve right away.

JBR'S SLOW COOKER BBQ RIBS

(GRAIN-, DAIRY-, EGG-, NUT-, SOY-FREE)

Good baby back ribs absolutely must come off the bone with ease. It is the cardinal rule of BBQ ribs, in fact. If you are still looking for ribs to write home about, these just might do the trick!

YIELD: 2 SERVINGS

FOR THE RIBS

1 tsp (3 g) sea salt

½ tsp ground pepper

¼ tsp onion powder

¼ tsp garlic powder

1 (3 ½ lb [1590 g]) rack pork baby back ribs

1 onion, thinly sliced

FOR THE BBQ SAUCE

½ cup (120 g) homemade ketchup (or high-quality store-bought)

¼ cup (60 ml) water

¼ cup (60 ml) pure maple syrup

¼ tsp liquid smoke

½ tsp onion powder

½ tsp garlic powder

¼ tsp paprika

FOR SERVING

Mashed "Taters" (page 101), optional

To make the ribs, sprinkle the salt, pepper, onion powder and garlic powder over the top of the rack of ribs. In a large slow cooker, arrange the rack of ribs with the top facing outward in a "C" shape, pressed against the side of the bowl. Turn the slow cooker on low and cook for about 6 hours. Times may vary slightly depending on slow cooker.

To make the BBQ sauce, combine all the sauce ingredients in a small saucepan and bring to a simmer over medium heat for 5 minutes.

Just before the ribs are finished cooking, preheat the oven to 325°F (170°C, or gas mark 3).

When the ribs are completely cooked, remove them from the slow cooker and lay them meat-side up on a foil-lined baking sheet. Spoon the sauce over the top, distributing it evenly. Bake for 35 minutes to allow the BBQ sauce to meld with the ribs. Remove the baking sheet from the oven carefully and serve. These are delicious paired with Mashed "Taters."

BLACKENED TILAPIA

(GRAIN-, DAIRY-, EGG-, NUT-, SOY-FREE)

You'd think this recipe came straight out of the Louisiana swamps, but with a few common seasonings and a cast-iron skillet, this Blackened Tilapia can easily become a household favorite. Laissez les bons temps rouler (let the good times roll)!!

YIELD: 5 SERVINGS

3 tbsp (45 ml) avocado oil (or preferred cooking fat)

1 tsp (3 g) paprika

1 tsp (3 g) dry mustard

1 tsp (3 g) cayenne pepper

1 tsp (3 g) cracked black pepper

½ tsp cumin

1 tsp (3 g) onion powder

1 tsp (3 g) garlic powder

½ tsp thyme

½ tsp oregano

1 tsp (3 g) sea salt

1 lb (454 g) wild caught tilapia fillets, fresh or frozen, thawed

Heat the oil in a cast-iron skillet over high heat. In a sandwich bag or bowl, combine all the seasonings until mixed well. Taking one fillet at a time, rub the seasoning into the fish on both sides. Once all the fillets are coated, fry in the hot oil on each side for about 3 minutes per side. Remove from the oil and serve.

CHEF'S TIP: Using a flexible spatula will aid in flipping the fish fillets over, as they can be very delicate once cooked.

SLOW COOKER BBQ PULLED CHICKEN

(GRAIN-, DAIRY-, EGG-, NUT-, SOY-FREE)

Making this homemade BBQ pulled chicken is as easy as sliding off a greasy log backwards. Toss these minimal ingredients into the slow cooker for flavorful chicken that falls apart faster than a hot knife through butter!

YIELD: 4 SERVINGS

½ large onion, diced

1 tsp (5 ml) avocado oil (or preferred cooking fat)

3 cloves garlic, minced

1 cup (240 g) organic tomato sauce

¼ cup (60 ml) local raw honey

1 tbsp (15 ml) Worcestershire sauce

2 tbsp (30 ml) apple cider vinegar

1 tsp (3 g) cracked black pepper

2 tsp (6 g) ground mustard

1 lb (454 g) organic chicken breasts

In a medium-size skillet, sauté the diced onion in the avocado oil over medium-high heat until nicely browned, about 10 minutes. Next add in the minced garlic and sauté for another 2 minutes. Now add in the tomato sauce, honey, Worcestershire sauce, apple cider vinegar, black pepper and ground mustard and stir until well combined. Bring to a simmer for 5 minutes, then remove from the heat.

Place the chicken breasts in the bottom of a medium-size slow cooker and turn on low. Pour the mixture over the top of the chicken and cook for 6 hours, or until the chicken shreds easily. Cooking times may vary depending on slow cooker.

CRAWFISH ÉTOUFÉE

(GRAIN-, DAIRY-, EGG-, SOY-FREE)

This creole favorite is no doubt Southern, tracking to the backwaters and swamps in Louisiana where crawfish are plentiful. While traditionally served with rice, this version uses zucchini "rice" to keep it grain-free, yet hearty nonetheless.

YIELD: 4 SERVINGS

FOR THE CRAWFISH ÉTOUFÉE

¼ cup (60 ml) olive oil (or preferred cooking fat)

2 tbsp (16 g) tapioca

2 tbsp (16 g) almond flour

2 tbsp (16 g) water chestnut flour

1 large onion, diced

3 celery stalks, diced

1 medium bell pepper, seeded and diced

4 cloves garlic, minced

1 cup (235 ml) beef stock

2 bay leaves

1 lb (454 g) crawfish tails (raw or cooked)

1 tsp (3 g) sea salt

½ tsp onion powder

1 tbsp (3 g) dried parsley

1 tsp (3 g) Cajun seasoning, or more to taste

FOR THE "RICE"

3 zucchini or yellow squash, spiral cut or julienned

1 tsp (5 ml) avocado oil (or preferred cooking fat)

½ tsp sea salt, or more to taste

FOR SERVING

Hot sauce (optional)

To make the crawfish étoufée: In a large, deep skillet combine the oil, tapioca, almond flour and water chestnut flour over medium-high heat. Stir the roux every few minutes until it turns a nice golden color, about 20–30 minutes. Once the desired color is achieved, add in the diced onion, celery and bell pepper. Cover the skillet (lifting to stir every few minutes) and allow to cook until the vegetables are tender and translucent, about another 8 minutes. Stirring will help prevent the roux from sticking to the skillet and burning, and help to incorporate it better into the vegetable mixture. Now add in the garlic, beef stock, bay leaves and crawfish tails and bring to a simmer. Add the sea salt, onion powder, parsley and Cajun seasoning. Stir regularly and allow the étoufée to thicken. Simmer for another 10 minutes while preparing your zucchini rice.

To make the rice, dice your spiral cut zucchini or yellow squash on a cutting board to the desired size. You can mince if you prefer a smaller "grain." Then, in a wok or large skillet, sauté your riced zucchini in the avocado oil and season with the sea salt. Cook over medium-high heat for about 10 minutes, or until the water has cooked out of the zucchini. Serve the étoufée over a scoop of squash "rice!" Add some hot sauce, if you'd like.

CRESCENT CITY SHRIMP + SAUSAGE GUMBO

(GRAIN-, DAIRY-, EGG-, SOY-FREE)

An authentic Louisiana gumbo starts with a dark, rich roux and ends with a savory, hearty Cajun kick. This version replaces the white flour and butter but still delivers that traditional gumbo flavor!

YIELD: 6 SERVINGS

2 tsp (6 g) finely ground water chestnut flour

2 tbsp (16 g) almond flour

2 tbsp (16 g) tapioca flour

¼ cup (60 g) bacon fat or lard

1 large onion, diced

1 green bell pepper, seeded and diced

2 celery stalks, diced

3 cloves garlic, minced

4 cups (940 ml) organic beef broth (homemade when possible)

2 cups (200 g) sliced okra

1 lb (454 g) raw peeled shrimp

1 lb (454 g) andouille sausage, sliced into 1" (2.5 cm) pieces

2 bay leaves

2 tbsp (30 ml) Worcestershire sauce

½ tsp Cajun seasoning

1 tsp (3 g) gumbo filé

Combine the flours and the fat in a large stockpot over medium-high heat. Stir the mixture continuously until it begins to darken, 20–30 minutes. Be careful not to burn the roux. Add the onion, green pepper, celery and garlic and cook with the roux until they soften, about 10–15 more minutes. Add the remaining ingredients and simmer for 20 minutes, or until the shrimp are cooked through and the okra is tender. Remove the bay leaves before serving.

CREAMY CAJUN CHICKEN + PASTA

(GRAIN-, DAIRY-, EGG-, SOY-FREE)

You'd never guess this dish was free of dairy with its creamy Cajun sauce, but it is! The tastiest trick you'll ever play on your taste buds, this meal balances the spice with the creamy sauce and the sweet potato noodles for a complex lil' number that will make you wanna party like it's Mardi Gras!

YIELD: 5 SERVINGS

1 lb (454 g) boneless organic chicken breasts

½ tsp white pepper, divided

2 tsp (6 g) paprika, divided

1 tsp (3 g) cayenne pepper, divided

2 tsp (6 g) onion powder, divided

2 tsp (6 g) garlic powder, divided

2 tsp (6 g) sea salt, divided (or more to taste)

2 tsp (2 g) dried parsley, divided

1 tsp (3 g) chili powder, divided

2 cups (300 g) cashews, soaked for 3 hours and drained

2 cups (470 ml) unsweetened flax milk (or other dairy-free milk)

2 sweet potatoes, spiral cut or julienned

1 tsp (5 ml) avocado oil (or preferred cooking fat)

Place the chicken breasts in the slow cooker and turn it on low. Sprinkle half the seasonings over the chicken breasts and allow to cook for 4 hours. To make the cream sauce, combine the cashews, flax milk and remaining half of the seasonings in a blender and puree until creamy. After the chicken has cooked for 4 hours, cut it into bite-size chunks and then pour the cream sauce over it in the slow cooker. Allow to cook for an additional hour on low.

In a skillet over high heat, cook the spiral cut sweet potatoes in the oil for about 10–15 minutes, or until softened. You'll want the water to evaporate from them but be careful not to overcook them if you prefer al dente "noodles." After the chicken is thoroughly cooked and the sauce is heated through, about 5 hours total, top the cooked sweet potato noodles with the chicken and sauce.

NEW ORLEANS JAMBALAYA

(GRAIN-, DAIRY-, NUT-, EGG-, SOY-FREE)

Another classic creole favorite, this jambalaya is spicy and satisfying! Made with sausage and shrimp, it is sure to please anyone in Crescent City and beyond! Prefer chicken instead? You can also substitute cooked cubed chicken for either of the protein options below.

YIELD: 4 SERVINGS

1 large onion, diced

1 large green bell pepper, seeded and diced

2 celery stalks, diced

2 tbsp (30 ml) bacon fat (or preferred cooking fat)

2 cloves garlic, minced

2 bay leaves

1 cup (235 ml) chicken broth

½ cup (90 g) chopped tomatoes

1 tbsp (8 g) Cajun seasoning

8 oz (227 g) peeled raw shrimp, fresh or frozen

8 oz (227 g) andouille sausage, sliced (substitute cooked cubed chicken if preferred)

1 tbsp (8 g) tapioca starch

FOR SERVING

Crawfish Étoufée's "rice" (page 71, optional)

In a large deep skillet, sauté the onion, bell pepper and celery in the bacon fat over high heat for 5 minutes, stirring occasionally. Add the garlic and bay leaves and cook for an additional 3 minutes. Next, add the broth and chopped tomatoes and bring to a boil. Sprinkle in the Cajun seasoning and stir to combine. Add the shrimp and sausage and bring back to a boil, cover and allow to cook for 15 minutes. Once the shrimp is cooked through, take 2 tablespoons (30 ml) of the broth and tomato mixture and ladle it into a small bowl. Mix in the tapioca starch to make a slurry and once well combined, spoon it back into the skillet for another 3 minutes, stir and serve. If desired, serve on top of the Crawfish Étoufée's "rice."

CAJUN CRAB FRIED "RICE"

(GRAIN-, DAIRY-, NUT-, SOY-, NIGHTSHADE-FREE)

Say it isn't so . . . fried "rice" made Cajun, with fresh lump crabmeat? It is so. It is so so good!
You will wonder why this dish never made it into your life before now!

YIELD: 4 SERVINGS

4 yellow squash, spiral cut or julienned and diced into rice-size pieces

1 onion, diced

1 tbsp (15 ml) avocado oil (or preferred cooking fat)

3 eggs

½ cup (75 g) peas, steamed

3 tbsp (6 g) minced fresh chives

3–4 tbsp (45–60 ml) coconut aminos

1 lb (454 g) fresh lump crabmeat, cooked

2 tsp (6 g) Cajun seasoning

In a large wok or deep skillet over medium-high heat, sauté the riced yellow squash and onion in the oil. This will take approximately 10 minutes for the moisture to be drawn out of the squash and onion and then evaporate. Once the water has evaporated, move the "rice" to one side of the wok, making space for the eggs. Scramble all 3 eggs for about 3–4 minutes, or until they are cooked through, then incorporate them into the "rice."

Next, add the peas and chives, stirring them both into the mixture. Drizzle the coconut aminos over the "rice" mixture and stir to combine. Now, add in the crabmeat and gently incorporate. Crab is delicate and can break apart easily, so take care in folding it into the wok. Last, season the crab fried "rice" with the Cajun seasoning. More can be added if a bolder flavor is preferred. Serve right away; it is best enjoyed fresh!

GULF COAST CRAB CHOWDER
WITH BACON + CHIVES

(GRAIN-, DAIRY-, EGG-, NUT-, SOY-FREE)

Fresh crab straight out of the Gulf is one of life's best indulgences. Add that crab to a steaming bowl
of hearty chowder, top it with crispy bacon and chives and you've got a little piece of paradise!
This chowder is dairy-free but thick and creamy just the same!

YIELD: 6 SERVINGS

---

5 tbsp (40 g) tapioca flour

5 tbsp (75 ml) olive oil

1 large onion, diced

1 celery stalk, diced

3 cloves garlic, crushed

1 small red bell pepper, seeded and diced

2 cups (470 ml) organic chicken broth

3 cups (705 ml) flax, almond or
coconut milk

¼ tsp black pepper

1 tsp (5 ml) hot pepper sauce

1 tbsp (15 ml) Worcestershire sauce or
coconut aminos

1 tsp (3 g) onion powder

Sea salt to taste

1 lb (454 g) fresh lump crabmeat

FOR SERVING

1 lb (454 g) cooked bacon, chopped

Handful of fresh chives, minced

In a deep stockpot, whisk together the tapioca flour and olive oil over medium-high heat for 3 minutes. Add in the onion, celery, garlic and red bell pepper and continue cooking until the vegetables soften, about 8 minutes. You will want to stir this mixture regularly as the flour mixture can easily stick to the pan if left unattended. Once the vegetables are softened, pour in the broth and milk. Stir well until any and all lumps are incorporated.

Add the black pepper, hot pepper sauce, Worcestershire, onion powder and sea salt. Bring to a simmer over high heat and allow to cook for about 30 minutes. Gently incorporate the lump crabmeat and stir. Crab is delicate and can break apart easily, so take care. Continue to cook on high for another 10 minutes, or until piping hot. Serve garnished with the crispy bacon and minced chives.

CHEF'S TIP: Love a biscuit with your chowder? See page 141 for the perfect accompaniment.

SIZZLIN' CHICKEN FAJITAS

(GRAIN-, DAIRY-, NUT-, EGG-, SOY-FREE)

Seasoned grilled chicken, onions and peppers sizzling on a cast-iron skillet basically embodies Tex-Mex in a single dish. With just the right balance of lime juice and cumin, this dish might have you wearing a sombrero before long!

YIELD: 4 SERVINGS

6 tbsp (90 ml) avocado oil (or preferred cooking fat), divided

Juice from 2 large limes

4 cloves garlic, minced

1 tsp (3 g) cumin

1 tsp (3 g) onion powder

1 tsp (3 g) sea salt

¼ tsp chili powder

½ tsp ground black pepper

1 lb (454 g) pastured chicken breasts, thinly sliced

1 large onion, thinly sliced

1 bell pepper, seeded and thinly sliced

FOR SERVING

Hearts of romaine

Combine 4 tablespoons (60 ml) of the oil, lime juice, garlic, cumin, onion powder, salt, chili powder and black pepper in a large zip-top plastic bag or a small casserole dish; shake or stir to combine well. Add the chicken, onion and bell pepper, cover the dish or close the bag, place in the fridge and let marinate for a minimum of 2 hours.

When ready to cook, heat the remaining 2 tablespoons (30 ml) oil in a cast-iron skillet or cast-iron griddle over medium-high heat. Remove the chicken, onion and pepper from the marinade and cook for about 5–8 minutes, or until the chicken is cooked through and the onions and peppers are softened. Remove from the skillet and serve with the hearts of romaine.

CHEF'S TIP: Alternatively you can make nachos by serving the fajitas on top of Tortilla Chips (page 187) or wrapped in soft Tortillas (page 189) for a more traditional feel.

SLOW COOKER
CREAMY CHIPOTLE CHICKEN

(GRAIN-, DAIRY-, EGG-, NUT-, SOY-FREE)

If that's not a mouthful I don't know what is! This recipe takes the heat of the chipotle peppers
in adobo sauce and cuts it with the dairy-free coconut cream. Shreds perfectly for tostadas
or tacos and will leave you craving more!

YIELD: 5 SERVINGS

2 lbs (908 g) organic boneless
chicken breasts

1 canned chipotle pepper (check adobo
ingredients for high-quality)

1 tbsp (15 ml) or more adobo sauce (from
the chipotle pepper can)

½ cup (120 ml) organic chicken broth
(homemade when possible)

2 tsp (6 g) minced garlic

1 cup (235 ml) coconut cream

FOR SERVING

Taco Shell (page 188, optional)

Tostada (page 188, optional)

½ cup (30 g) chopped cilantro, optional

Place the chicken breasts in the bottom of your slow cooker and turn the heat on low. In a blender, puree the chipotle pepper, adobo sauce, chicken broth and garlic. Spoon on top of the chicken and allow to cook for around 4-5 hours. Add the coconut cream and allow to cook for an additional 30 minutes to 1 hour more, or until the chicken shreds easily. Serve in a Taco Shell or a Tostada, sprinkled with cilantro, if that strikes your fancy!

DIXIE TUNA CASSEROLE

(GRAIN-, DAIRY-, NUT-, EGG-, SOY-, NIGHTSHADE-FREE)

You won't find any egg noodles or breadcrumbs in this version of the Southern favorite,
but you might be surprised at how reminiscent it is of the old classic!

YIELD: 6 SERVINGS

8 oz (227 g) button mushrooms, diced

2 tbsp (30 ml) olive oil, divided

¼ tsp herbs de Provence

¼ tsp sea salt

¼ tsp garlic powder

¼ tsp onion powder

2 cups (470 ml) organic chicken or beef broth (homemade when possible), divided

2 tbsp (16 g) tapioca or arrowroot flour

15 oz (420 g) green peas

14 oz (392 g) eco-friendly tuna fish, drained

1 large sweet onion, spiral cut or julienned

1 cup (70 g) crushed organic or homemade sweet potato chips or white potato chips

In a medium-size saucepan, sauté the diced mushrooms in 1 tablespoon (15 ml) of the oil over high heat for about 10 minutes. Once they are nicely browned and the water has evaporated from the saucepan, season with the herbs de Provence, sea salt, garlic powder and onion powder. Pour in 1 ¾ cups (411 ml) of the broth. Whisk the tapioca into the remaining ¼ cup (60 ml) broth until there are no lumps. Slowly whisk the slurry into the stockpot of mushrooms and broth, whisking to combine well. Bring the mixture to a boil over high heat and cook for about 10 minutes, or until it thickens. Remove from the heat and fold in the peas and tuna. Set aside.

Preheat the oven to 350°F (180°C, or gas mark 4).

In the same skillet, add the remaining 1 tablespoon (15 ml) oil and sauté the onion strings over high heat. Stir the onions periodically for about 10–15 minutes, or until they are nicely browned; these will serve as the base of your casserole. Once the onions are browned, transfer them to a greased 2-quart (2-L) casserole dish and distribute them evenly on the bottom of the dish. Spoon in the tuna mixture and distribute it evenly as well. Lastly, top the casserole with the crushed chips. Bake for about 20 minutes, or until the top is nicely browned.

CRISPY BEEF TACOS

(GRAIN-, DAIRY-, NUT-, EGG-, SOY-FREE)

Amigos! This is the Tex-Mex food that started it all. And to be quite honest, it is the most valuable
and hardest to give up when purging the grain. At long last there is a crispy taco recipe that
will have your gringo friends convinced you are from Tejas!

YIELD: 4 SERVINGS

FOR THE TACO MEAT

1 lb (454 g) grass-fed ground beef

½ onion, diced

½ tsp chili powder

¼ tsp cumin

¼ tsp garlic powder

¼ tsp onion powder

¼ tsp dried parsley

¼ tsp paprika

¼ tsp sea salt

FOR SERVING

4 Taco Shells (page 188) or substitute
hearts of romaine

1 cup (70 g) shredded lettuce

½ cup (50 g) diced black olives

½ cup (80 g) minced red onion

½ cup (30 g) chopped cilantro

½ cup (80 g) diced tomatoes

Dairy-free sour cream (optional)

To prepare the taco meat, cook the beef and onion in a large skillet over high heat for about 8 minutes, or until it is no longer pink. Add in the seasonings and stir to combine, then remove the skillet from the heat.

To assemble the tacos, take a shell or heart of romaine and spoon a couple tablespoons (30 g) of the meat mixture into it. Then sprinkle on the lettuce, olives, red onion, cilantro and tomatoes, and dollop with dairy-free sour cream, if desired. All toppings can be substituted for other preferred toppings, depending on taste and/or food sensitivities.

PALEO CHICKEN CHIMICHANGAS

(GRAIN-, DAIRY-, EGG-, NUT-, SOY-FREE)

If you've ever tasted this most delectable Tex-Mex dish, you know it is a delicious, crispy envelope wrapped around a hot, savory filling. This version is filled with seasoned chicken and is perfect paired with fresh salsa or Chile con Queso (page 132)!

YIELD: 4 SERVINGS

4 large Tortillas (page 189) or substitute hearts of romaine

FOR THE FILLING

1 lb (454 g) pastured organic chicken breast

1 onion, diced

2 cloves garlic, minced

½ tsp sea salt

¼ tsp cumin

¼ tsp chili powder

½ tsp dried parsley

¼ tsp freshly cracked black pepper

1 tbsp (15 ml) avocado oil, plus more for frying

FOR SERVING

Homemade Salsa (page 128)

Dairy-free sour cream

Chopped fresh cilantro

To make the tortillas, follow the recipe on page 189 but only bake them for 8–10 minutes, or until they "set." They should not be cooked through as they will crack when folding. They can be made ahead, frozen and thawed or made fresh, depending on your preference.

Preheat the oven to 350°F (180°C, or gas mark 4).

To make the filling, in a skillet, cook the chicken, onion, seasonings and oil over medium-high heat for about 15 minutes, or until the chicken is cooked through. Turn the chicken over halfway through, to ensure both sides are nicely browned. Remove from the heat and cut into bite-size pieces.

Scoop about ½ cup (70 g) of the chicken mixture into each tortilla. Fold the two opposing edges in toward the center, then roll like a burrito, starting from one of the open ends to the other. If the dough cracks, seal it back together by hand. Because you are only par-baking them, they should still be doughy enough to re-seal. Place the folded chimichangas, seam-side down, on a parchment-lined baking sheet and bake for about 5 minutes to seal the dough shut. The underneath should resemble an envelope folded over and sealed.

Remove from the oven, transfer to a skillet with some oil and fry each chimichanga over medium-high heat for a few minutes on each side, or until nicely browned. Serve with fresh salsa, dairy-free sour cream and fresh cilantro.

STUFFED POBLANO PEPPERS

(GRAIN-, DAIRY-, EGG-, SOY-FREE)

Another Tex-Mex favorite, stuffed poblano peppers can be made with a variety of fillings and are usually smothered with cheese. For these, a creamy cashew cheese replaces the dairy yet still bakes up toasty and delicious!

YIELD: 5 SERVINGS

FOR THE CASHEW CHEESE

½ cup (75 g) cashews, soaked for 3 hours and drained

½ cup (120 ml) full-fat coconut milk

½ tsp sea salt

¼ tsp onion powder

½ tsp dried parsley

FOR THE POBLANO PEPPERS AND FILLING

1 lb (454 g) organic grass-fed ground beef

1 onion, diced

4 cloves garlic, minced

½ tsp chili powder

½ tsp cumin

1 tsp (3 g) sea salt

¾ cup (180 g) organic tomato sauce

5 poblano peppers, sliced in half vertically and seeded

To make the cashew cheese, puree the cashews, coconut milk, sea salt, onion powder and dried parsley in a blender on medium speed until creamy and void of lumps. Set aside.

Preheat the oven to 350°F (180°C, or gas mark 4).

To make the peppers and filling, sauté the ground beef and diced onion in a large skillet over high heat for about 5 minutes. Add the garlic, chili powder, cumin, sea salt and tomato sauce and cook for another 5–10 minutes, or until the meat is cooked through and the seasonings are well incorporated, stirring occasionally.

Stuff approximately ¼ cup (60 g) of the meat mixture into each pepper half. Set your open-faced, stuffed pepper onto a foil-lined baking sheet and repeat until all 10 halves are filled with meat. Next, spoon the cashew cheese on top of the meat, 1–2 tablespoons (15–30 g) per pepper. Bake for 25 minutes, or until heated through.

TEXAS GRILLED RIB EYES + MARINADE

(GRAIN-, DAIRY-, NUT-, EGG-, SOY-, NIGHTSHADE-FREE)

A juicy seared steak off the grill is no joke down South. Either you "got it" or you don't. This marinade helps make any steak tender and incredibly flavorful, so if you want to look like a pro, look no further!

YIELD: 2 SERVINGS

3 tbsp (24 g) minced garlic

¼ cup (60 ml) coconut aminos

3 tbsp (45 ml) lemon juice

1 tbsp (4 g) chopped parsley

1 tsp (3 g) black pepper

⅓ cup (80 ml) olive oil (or preferred cooking fat)

1 tsp (3 g) onion powder

3 tbsp (45 ml) high-quality Worcestershire sauce

2 grass-fed rib-eye steaks (8–9 oz [227–252 g] each)

Combine all the ingredients except for the steaks in a mixing bowl. Whisk vigorously until well blended. In a shallow glass casserole dish, arrange the steaks so that they are not touching, and then pour the marinade over the top. Cover and refrigerate for a minimum of 2 hours.

When the steaks are ready, preheat the grill to high heat.

Transfer the steaks to the grill; once they are placed, the steaks should not be moved until they are ready to be flipped. This typically takes anywhere from 6–8 minutes, depending on how well done they are preferred. After 6–8 minutes, use tongs to flip them over for another 6–8 minutes. Using a fork to flip them can release the juices that are vital to a moist, tender steak, so tongs are preferred. Once the steaks have been cooked on both sides, you may slice into one of them to confirm they are cooked to preference.

ON
THE SIDE

Growing up, my grandma used to take me out for supper after we saw the seasonal ballet or matinee play together. I could make an entire meal out of side dishes from mashed potatoes to greens. There was something so comforting 'bout that plate filled with fixin's that I never missed the main course!

While Southern food conjures up images of fried chicken and pies, the truth is that the side dishes sometimes make the meal. In this chapter, I've got you covered from Fried Green Tomatoes (page 102) and Squash Casserole (page 94) to Mashed "Taters" (page 101) and Deep South Grain-Free Grits (page 95), so you'll find a little of everything to decorate your plate.

SOULFUL COLLARD GREENS
+ CRISPED BACON

(GRAIN-, DAIRY-, NUT-, EGG-, SOY-, NIGHTSHADE-FREE)

Collard greens are the quintessential soul food. In the South it seems everybody's got a family recipe that's been passed down through the years, but whatever the version, it is a Southern staple if there ever was one. This recipe calls for bacon, and lots of it, for a hearty flavor that will get anyone to eat their greens! This side makes a perfect accompaniment to Mama's Fried Chicken (page 35).

YIELD: 4 SERVINGS

12 oz (336 g) organic, pastured bacon

1 bunch collard greens (approximately 8 oz [227 g])

1 large onion, diced

3 cloves garlic, minced

½ tsp sea salt

2 cups (470 ml) organic chicken broth (homemade when possible)

Preheat the oven to 375°F (190°C, or gas mark 5).

Place the strips of bacon on a large foil-lined baking sheet and bake for about 30 minutes, or until the bacon is crispy. Remove the bacon from the oven once it's finished cooking and carefully pour off the bacon drippings into a deep stockpot. Set the bacon aside.

While the bacon is baking, clean the collard greens and pull the leaves off of the large central spine. Tear the leaves into smaller bite-size pieces by hand and set aside.

In the stock pot, sauté the diced onion in the bacon fat over medium-high heat, stirring occasionally, until they are nicely browned, approximately 15 minutes. Toss in the minced garlic and collard greens. Cook the collard greens until wilted, about 4 minutes, and then add the salt and chicken broth. Cover the stockpot and allow to simmer for about 40 minutes, or until the greens are nice and tender. Crumble the cooled bacon on top of the collard greens and serve.

SQUASH CASSEROLE

(GRAIN-, DAIRY-, SOY-, NIGHTSHADE-FREE)

When I was younger my family ate frequently at a restaurant that was absolutely famous for its squash casserole. Who knew squash could be so addictive?! With its buttery and slightly sweet charm, it was certainly worth making into a dairy-free, grain-free version!

YIELD: 8 SERVINGS

---

1 large Vidalia onion, diced

2 tbsp (30 ml) avocado oil (or preferred cooking fat)

3 tbsp (36 g) maple sugar or coconut sugar

3 medium-size yellow squash, ends removed and coarsely chopped

2 eggs

1 tsp sea salt, divided

¼ tsp cracked black pepper

1 cup (150 g) pecan pieces

Preheat the oven to 350°F (180°C, or gas mark 4). Grease a casserole dish.

In a medium-size skillet, sauté the diced onion in the oil over medium-high heat, stirring occasionally so they do not burn, until they brown nicely, around 10–15 minutes. Add the maple sugar and cook for 5 more minutes.

While your onions are browning, boil the squash in a medium-size saucepan with enough water to cover for about 10 minutes, or until fork-tender. Remove the squash from the heat, drain and mash with a potato masher or a fork. Add the onions, eggs, ½ teaspoon of the sea salt and the black pepper. Pour the mixture into the prepared casserole dish.

Combine the pecan pieces with the remaining ½ teaspoon sea salt. Sprinkle the pecans over the squash and bake for 30 minutes, uncovered. If you would like the pecans to toast a little more, you can increase the heat for the last 5 minutes or so to 425°F (220°C, or gas mark 7), but watch carefully or the nuts can burn. Remove from the oven after a total of 30 minutes bake time and serve hot!

DEEP SOUTH GRAIN-FREE GRITS

(GRAIN-, DAIRY-, EGG-, NUT-, SOY-, NIGHTSHADE-FREE)

Okay, let's chat for a second. The secret to good Southern grits means the perfect balance between corn, dairy and extra dairy. That just will not work when eating without grain or dairy, will it? These grits are the best substitute in town thanks to proper seasoning and healthy alternatives!

YIELD: 6 SERVINGS

1 head cauliflower, chopped into florets

½ onion, minced

1 tbsp (15 ml) olive oil (or preferred cooking fat)

1 cup (235 ml) organic chicken broth (homemade when possible)

⅓ cup (80 ml) flax milk (or other dairy-free milk)

½ tsp sea salt, or more to taste

½ tsp ground black pepper

½ tsp onion powder

1 tsp (3 g) arrowroot, tapioca or water chestnut flour

FOR SERVING

Crisped bacon

Dairy-Free Butter (page 141)

In a food processor or blender, mince the cauliflower florets on low speed in small batches to avoid leaving behind big chunks. In a large, deep skillet, sauté the minced onion in the oil over high heat until translucent, about 8 minutes. Add the "riced" cauliflower to the skillet and sauté over high heat for about 10 minutes.

Add the chicken broth and cook for 5 more minutes over high heat. Using an immersion blender on the low setting, blend sporadic sections of the cauliflower mixture. You do not want a true puree, as grain-based grits do have some texture. Lower the heat to medium and add the flax milk, salt, pepper and onion powder. Stir well and then sprinkle in the flour, making sure to distribute it evenly. Allow the grits to cook for about 5–8 more minutes, until the desired texture is reached. If you would like them pureed more, you can use the immersion blender at any time. If they need to be thinned out more, you can add in more chicken broth or flax milk, depending on your preference. These are best served with an extra sprinkle of pepper and salt, crisped bacon and Dairy-Free Butter.

GREEN BEAN CASSEROLE

(GRAIN-, DAIRY-, NUT-, EGG-, SOY-, NIGHTSHADE-FREE)

The word casserole must have its origins in some great-great-great-grandma's Southern kitchen, right?
Mastered for generations, green bean casserole is not just a Thanksgiving staple, it is a year-round favorite.
This recipe uses arrowroot for thickening and for frying the onions, so you won't find
any unnecessary grain or gluten here!

YIELD: 8 SERVINGS

FOR THE CASSEROLE

1 lb (454 g) white mushrooms, chopped

1 onion, diced

2 tbsp (30 ml) olive oil (or preferred cooking fat)

4 cups (940 ml) organic beef broth (homemade when possible)

1 tbsp (8 g) herbs de Provence

½ tsp sea salt

1 tsp (3 g) cracked black pepper

1 tsp (1 g) dried parsley

¼ cup (60 ml) full-fat coconut milk (or preferred dairy-free milk)

3–4 tbsp (24–32 g) arrowroot flour

1 lb (454 g) French green beans (the thin ones), trimmed and steamed

FOR THE ONION TOPPING

1 onion, thinly sliced

¼ cup (60 ml) full-fat coconut milk

½ tsp sea salt

½ tsp pepper

¼ tsp garlic powder

½ cup (60 g) arrowroot flour

½ cup (60 g) potato starch

¼ cup (60 ml) lard (or preferred cooking fat)

Preheat the oven to 350°F (180°C, or gas mark 4).

To make the casserole, in a large stockpot, sauté the mushrooms and diced onion in the olive oil over high heat for about 5 minutes, covered. Remove the lid and allow the vegetables to cook for another 5 minutes. Add the broth and seasonings and bring to a boil. Lower the heat and simmer for 10 minutes. Remove from the heat and puree the soup in a blender, adding in the coconut milk. Once the ingredients are well blended, return back to the stockpot and raise the heat to high. In a small bowl, make a slurry with ¼ cup (60 ml) of the soup mixture and the arrowroot flour. Stir well to combine, then return the slurry to the stockpot.

Bring the soup to a simmer for 5 minutes while you transfer your steamed green beans to a casserole dish. Ladle 4 cups (940 ml) of the mushroom soup over the green beans and bake for 30 minutes. You will have a little of the soup left over and can eat it as a soup or use it as a gravy.

To make the onion topping, while the casserole bakes, place the sliced onion in a large zip-top bag. Pour the coconut milk into the bag, seal the top and shake to coat the onion. Next sprinkle in the seasonings, arrowroot flour and potato starch. Seal the top and shake again to coat the onion slices with flour.

In a skillet, heat the cooking fat over high heat and fry the onion slices until nicely browned, about 8 minutes, stirring and flipping them to brown all sides. Once the casserole has baked for 30 minutes, remove the dish from the oven and top with the browned onions. Return the casserole to the oven once again and bake for an additional 10 minutes. Serve warm.

OVEN-CRISPED BRUSSELS SPROUTS

(GRAIN-, DAIRY-, NUT-, EGG-, SOY-, NIGHTSHADE-FREE)

If it's been a while since you gave Brussels sprouts a try, now's the time! These combine stone-ground mustard and pure maple syrup for a flavor explosion that makes even the littlest cowfolk kick up their heels!

YIELD: 4 SERVINGS

12 oz (340 g) Brussels sprouts

3 tbsp (45 ml) pure maple syrup

3 tbsp (45 ml) olive oil

1 tbsp (15 g) stone-ground mustard

1 tsp (3 g) garlic powder

½ tsp sea salt

Preheat the oven to 375°F (190°C, or gas mark 5).

Slice the brown ends off of the Brussels sprouts. In a bag or bowl with a lid, combine all the ingredients and shake well to coat. Pour the contents onto a foil-lined baking sheet and bake for 25–30 minutes, or until starting to brown and crisp. Remove from the oven and serve hot.

ROASTED ASPARAGUS
WITH MAPLE BALSAMIC GLAZE

(GRAIN-, DAIRY-, NUT-, EGG-, SOY-, NIGHTSHADE-FREE)

Believe it or not, we Southerners love our greens just as much as our "frieds." This roasted asparagus
is simple to toss together and combines the sweet of the maple with the savory of the balsamic and garlic.
It's one side dish that might just take center stage!

YIELD: 4 SERVINGS

1 bunch asparagus (about 1 lb [454 g]),
washed

2 tbsp (30 ml) olive oil

½ tsp sea salt

½ tsp ground black pepper

FOR THE MAPLE BALSAMIC GLAZE

½ cup (120 ml) balsamic vinegar

1 tbsp (15 ml) pure maple syrup

2 tbsp (30 ml) coconut oil, melted

3 cloves garlic, minced

Preheat the oven to 400°F (200°C, or gas mark 6).

On a baking sheet spread the asparagus out and drizzle the olive oil evenly over the
top. Next sprinkle the sea salt and pepper over the asparagus. Bake for 20 minutes, or
until the asparagus spears are slightly tender but still firm.

While the asparagus is in the oven, combine the balsamic vinegar, maple syrup and
coconut oil in a small saucepan over medium-high and simmer for about 12 minutes.
Add in the garlic and stir and simmer for 3 additional minutes.

The glaze should be able to be drizzled over the top of the asparagus without being
too runny or too thick. Test the consistency and remove from the heat when the
desired consistency is reached, about 15 minutes total. Serve the asparagus warm
drizzled with the maple balsamic glaze.

MASHED "TATERS"

(GRAIN-, DAIRY-, EGG-, NUT-, SOY-, NIGHTSHADE-FREE)

There is no shame in the potato game, but if you are sensitive to nightshades, try this mashed tater recipe!
Delicious starchy goodness, perfect for smotherin' in the gravy of your pickin'!

YIELD: 4 SERVINGS

1 lb (454 g) yuca root, peeled and coarsely chopped

¼ cup (60 ml) flax milk (or preferred dairy-free milk)

2 tbsp (30 ml) avocado oil (or preferred cooking fat)

½ tsp sea salt

½ tsp black pepper

½ tsp garlic powder

¼ tsp onion powder

Coconut flour, as needed (optional)

FOR SERVING

Cream Gravy (page 42)

Fill a stockpot with water and bring to a boil over high heat. Add the yuca and boil for 20–25 minutes, or until fork-tender. Drain the water and remove the yuca from the pot. Remove the woody core once the yuca is cool enough to handle.

In a mixing bowl, combine the yuca, flax milk, oil and seasonings and mash with a potato masher until the desired consistency is reached. Yuca is slightly stickier than potato, so be cautious of over-mashing. If the yuca is stickier than preferred, add 1 teaspoon (3 g) of coconut flour at a time until the desired texture is achieved. Use the coconut flour sparingly, as it can be gritty if overused. Serve warm with Cream Gravy.

★ SEE PAGE 90 FOR IMAGE.

FRIED GREEN TOMATOES

(GRAIN-, DAIRY-, NUT-, SOY-FREE)

In case you hadn't heard, Fried Green Tomatoes is not just a classic Southern film; it's also a classic Southern dish. This version nixes the white flour and creates a delicate, yet crispy breading that is sure to be a crowd-pleaser!

YIELD: 2 SERVINGS

1 egg

½ cup (120 ml) full-fat coconut milk

½ cup (60 g) tapioca flour

3 tbsp (24 g) coconut flour

½ tsp garlic sea salt

Lard, avocado oil or coconut oil for frying

1 large organic green tomato

FOR SERVING

Ranch Dressing (page 131)

Crack the egg into a bowl and whisk in the coconut milk. On a clean plate, combine the tapioca flour, coconut flour and garlic sea salt until well incorporated.

Heat the cooking fat over medium-high heat in a large, deep skillet. You'll want just enough oil to coat the bottom of the pan; it is not necessary to deep-fry these. Carefully slice your tomato into ⅓- to ½-inch (8 mm to 1.3 cm) slices with a knife or mandoline. Now take one tomato slice and coat both sides in the egg wash. Then dredge it in the flour mixture until it is coated evenly on both sides. You may choose to repeat the egg wash and flour coat if you want to have a thicker crust. Repeat with each tomato slice and set aside for frying.

Once your oil is hot enough (look for it to shimmer), fry a few tomato slices at a time, depending on the size of your skillet. Be careful not to overcrowd your tomatoes as this will make flipping them difficult. Once nicely browned on each side, remove the tomato slices and place them on a towel-lined plate to absorb excess oil. Alternatively, you can omit the egg. The tomatoes will not crisp up identically to the egg version, but they are still tasty with this omission! Serve warm with Ranch Dressing.

SWEET POTATO CASSEROLE
+ CRISPY FRIED ONIONS

(GRAIN-, DAIRY-, NUT-, SOY-FREE)

Sweet potato casserole is perfect for the holidays or just a traditional down-home family dinner.
This one is topped with crispy fried onions for an extra mouthwatering rendition and pairs perfectly with the
Blackened Tilapia (page 69).

YIELD: 8 SERVINGS

FOR THE CASSEROLE

2 large sweet potatoes

1 cup (235 ml) full-fat coconut milk,
or more as needed

2 eggs

1 tsp (3 g) sea salt

3 cloves garlic, minced

½ tsp freshly cracked black pepper

¼ tsp paprika

¼ tsp dry mustard

FOR THE ONION TOPPING

¼ cup (60 ml) avocado oil, lard or coconut
oil for frying

1 egg

¼ cup (60 ml) full-fat coconut milk,
flax milk or almond milk

⅓ cup (40 g) water chestnut flour

½ tsp sea salt

1 medium onion, cut into rings

Preheat the oven to 350°F (180°C, or gas mark 4).

To make the casserole, clean and peel the sweet potatoes, then slice them into ⅛-inch (3 mm) slices. Layer them in a 9 x 9-inch (23 x 23-cm) casserole dish. Mix together the coconut milk, eggs and seasonings in a bowl. Whisk well to combine. Pour the mixture evenly over the layered sweet potatoes. Bake, uncovered, for 40 minutes.

To make the onion topping, while the sweet potatoes are baking, heat the oil in a medium-size skillet over high heat. Whisk together the egg and coconut milk in a bowl. On a clean plate, combine the water chestnut flour and salt. Coat the sliced onions in the egg wash, then dredge in the flour mixture on both sides until evenly coated. Fry the onions until lightly browned and then set aside. If you need to fry in batches, add more oil if necessary between batches. Do not overcook the onions, as they will continue to bake on top of the casserole.

Remove the sweet potatoes from oven after 40 minutes and top them with the fried onions. Bake for 20 more minutes, or until the onions are crisped and the potatoes are tender.

ROUGHAGE

Roughage isn't just for rabbits! These Southern salads are so flavorful and amazingly delicious, you'll forget they are nutritious as well. If you've ever assumed salads were boring, these are for you.

Oftentimes the Paleo lifestyle is accused of being meat-centric. But the truth is, veggies and salads are a major focus of the daily nutrient load. The Tex-Mex Taco Salad + Chipotle Ranch Dressing (page 115) and the Southern Spinach Salad + Warm Bacon Vinaigrette (page 111) are just two of the salads featured that will make your taste buds sing and help you celebrate greens more than ever!

TRAIL MIX TUNA SALAD

(GRAIN-, DAIRY-, SOY-, NIGHTSHADE-FREE)

It's no secret: sometimes simple is just plain better. There are times for investing kitchen in prep and there are times to get a tasty, nutritious meal on the table with efficiency and ease. I grew up with crunch in my tuna salad, giving it texture and personality. This Trail Mix Tuna Salad is reminiscent of that childhood favorite! When selecting a trail mix, try avoiding peanuts and over-sugared mixes; keep it simple and clean!

YIELD: 2 SERVINGS

3–4 tbsp (45–60 ml) homemade mayonnaise (or high-quality store-bought)

2 (5-oz [140-g]) cans sustainably caught tuna fish

½ cup (75 g) trail mix of your choice with good-quality nuts, seeds and dried fruit

FOR SERVING

Mixed greens or Tostadas (page 188)

In a bowl, mix the mayonnaise into the tuna fish first, and then incorporate the trail mix. Do not overmix. Serve on a bed of mixed greens or on a Tostada.

FAMILY SECRET CHICKEN SALAD

(GRAIN-, DAIRY-, SOY-, NIGHTSHADE-FREE)

Chicken salad recipes are like the crowned jewels of the South. They are coveted and they are kept quiet!
Make this rendition and people will swear you've gotten ahold of a secret family recipe!

YIELD: 5 SERVINGS

2 tbsp (30 ml) bacon fat (or preferred cooking fat)

1 lb (454 g) organic boneless chicken breasts

1 tsp (3 g) sea salt, divided

½ tsp pepper, divided

½ onion, diced

½ cup (75 g) pecans, chopped

1 Granny Smith apple, cored and diced

½ cup (120 ml) homemade mayonnaise (or high-quality store-bought)

FOR SERVING

Your choice of greens

Sweet Potato Slider Buns (page 146)

In a large skillet or wok, heat the oil over high heat. Place the chicken breasts in the hot oil and season them with half of the salt and pepper on the side facing up. After 5 minutes, flip the breasts over, season the alternate side with the remaining salt and pepper and add the diced onion to the skillet.

Once the chicken breasts are completely cooked through, remove them from the skillet and cut them up into bite-size pieces. Place the chicken, pecans and apple in a mixing bowl. Leave the onions in the skillet until they are nicely browned, then remove them as well and add them to the mixing bowl. Stir in the mayonnaise until all ingredients are well combined. Serve on top of a bed of greens or on a Sweet Potato Slider Bun.

SOUTHERN SPINACH SALAD + WARM BACON VINAIGRETTE

(GRAIN-, DAIRY-, EGG-, NUT-, SOY-, NIGHTSHADE-FREE)

I remember my mom ordering this salad when I was younger, and although I didn't quite appreciate the tangy, salty, flavorful dressing back then, I now realize its magical powers! Served while the dressing is still warm, this salad is truly like no other.

YIELD: 4 SERVINGS

8 slices bacon

½ onion, diced

¼ tsp ground black pepper

¼ tsp garlic powder

1 tbsp (12 g) coconut palm sugar

¼ cup (60 ml) olive oil

1 tbsp (15 ml) apple cider vinegar

1 tbsp (15 ml) red wine vinaigrette

7 oz (198 g) organic baby spinach

Preheat the oven to 375°F (190°C, or gas mark 5).

Arrange the bacon strips on a foil-lined baking sheet and bake for about 20–25 minutes, or until crispy. Carefully remove the baking sheet from the oven and reserve the bacon drippings. Chop the cooked bacon and set aside.

In a small skillet, heat the bacon drippings over high heat and add the diced onion, black pepper and garlic powder. Cook until the onions start to brown slightly, about 10–12 minutes. Remove the onions from the heat, add them to the chopped bacon in a large mixing bowl and then stir in the coconut sugar, olive oil, apple cider vinegar and red wine vinaigrette. Fold in the baby spinach and toss to coat. Serve while the dressing is still warm.

COBB SALAD + MAPLE VINAIGRETTE

(GRAIN-, DAIRY-, NUT-, SOY-FREE)

Cobb salads are the perfect feast, especially during hot Southern summers. Packed with grilled chicken, avocado, fresh juicy tomato and bacon, this salad meets all your needs in one tasty bowl!

YIELD: 4 SERVINGS

FOR THE VINAIGRETTE

½ cup (120 ml) olive oil

¼ cup (60 ml) avocado oil

¼ cup (60 ml) red wine vinegar

½ tsp dry mustard

2 cloves garlic, minced

¼ tsp black pepper

¼ tsp sea salt

1 tbsp (15 ml) pure maple syrup

1 tsp (1 g) dried parsley

Juice from ½ lemon

FOR THE SALAD

3 hearts of romaine, coarsely chopped

12 oz (340 g) cooked pastured bacon, chopped

1 lb (454 g) grilled organic chicken breast, sliced into bite-size pieces

1 large organic tomato, seeded and diced

3 hard-boiled eggs, diced

1 large avocado, pitted and diced

To make the vinaigrette, in a salad dressing cruet, shake up the vinaigrette ingredients. You may chill the dressing while preparing the salad, to allow the flavors to marry.

To make the salad, in a large salad serving bowl, layer the chopped hearts of romaine in the bottom of the bowl. Then in a single row on top of the romaine, arrange the chopped bacon. Repeat with the chicken, tomato, eggs and avocado. Serve with the vinaigrette right away.

TEX-MEX TACO SALAD + CHIPOTLE RANCH DRESSING

(GRAIN-, DAIRY-, NUT-, SOY-FREE)

This salad is so satisfying you won't even miss the fried tortilla bowl! And try not to be embarrassed when you have to make a second batch of chipotle ranch: it's just that addictive.

YIELD: 4 SERVINGS

FOR THE TACO MEAT

1 lb (454g) grass-fed ground beef

½ onion, diced

½ tsp chili powder

¼ tsp cumin

¼ tsp garlic powder

¼ tsp onion powder

¼ tsp dried parsley

¼ tsp paprika

¼ tsp sea salt

FOR THE CHIPOTLE RANCH DRESSING

⅓ cup (80 ml) homemade mayonnaise (or high-quality store-bought)

¼ cup (60 ml) flax milk (or other dairy-free milk)

1 tsp (1 g) minced fresh dill

1 tsp (1 g) minced fresh chives

¼ tsp sea salt

¼ tsp pepper

¼ tsp garlic powder

¼ tsp onion powder

¼ tsp parsley

Juice from ½ small lemon

1 tsp (5 ml) adobo sauce (good quality)

½ chipotle pepper in adobo sauce

FOR THE SALAD

12 oz (340 g) organic romaine hearts, chopped

½ cup (50 g) diced black olives

½ cup (80 g) minced red onion

½ cup (30 g) chopped cilantro

Dairy-free sour cream (optional)

(continued)

TEX-MEX TACO SALAD +
CHIPOTLE RANCH DRESSING (CONTINUED)

To make the taco meat, cook the beef and onion in a large skillet over high heat for about 8 minutes, or until the meat is no longer pink. Add in the seasonings and stir to combine, then remove the skillet from the heat.

To make the dressing, combine all the ingredients in a blender and blend until well combined. The consistency should be creamy.

To make the salad, either divide the chopped romaine into 4 equal portions or place into 1 large serving bowl. If divided, also divide the taco meat and toppings, then drizzle with the chipotle ranch. If preparing in a large serving bowl, top the romaine with all of the taco meat, then sprinkle the olives, red onion and cilantro and a dollop of dairy-free sour cream, if desired. All toppings can be substituted for other preferred toppings, depending on taste and/or food sensitivities.

STRAWBERRY FIELDS SALAD WITH CANDIED PECANS + BLUEBERRY VINAIGRETTE

(GRAIN-, DAIRY-, EGG-, SOY-, NIGHTSHADE-FREE)

Southerners can make just about anything "candied"—pecans, yams and probably even fried chicken! What makes this salad even better than the candied pecans and blueberry vinaigrette that dress it is that there is not a lick of refined sugar to be found!

YIELD: 4 SERVINGS

FOR THE CANDIED PECANS

8 oz (227 g) pecan halves

¼ cup (60 ml) local honey

FOR THE BLUEBERRY VINAIGRETTE

6 oz (170 g) organic blueberries

½ cup (120 ml) balsamic vinegar

2 tbsp (30 ml) local raw honey

Zest from 1 lemon

¼ cup (60 ml) olive oil

¼ tsp onion powder

¼ tsp garlic powder

¼ tsp sea salt

¼ tsp ground black pepper

FOR THE SALAD

7 oz (198 g) organic mixed field greens

1 cup (170 g) sliced organic strawberries

To make the candied pecans, preheat the toaster oven (a conventional oven may also be used) to 350°F (180°C, or gas mark 4) and line a baking sheet with parchment paper. Spread the pecans evenly over the parchment paper and drizzle with the local honey. Bake for about 10 minutes, watching carefully so they do not burn. Remove them from the toaster oven and set aside to cool. The honey will cool and crystallize over the pecans.

To make the blueberry vinaigrette, place the blueberries, balsamic vinegar, honey and lemon zest in a small saucepan over medium-high heat and cook for about 10 minutes, crushing the blueberries as they soften. Remove the blueberry mixture from the heat and press it through a sieve or fine-mesh strainer. Combine the strained blueberry vinegar with the olive oil, onion powder, garlic powder, salt and pepper in a salad dressing cruet or shaker. Shake vigorously until the ingredients are well combined.

To make the salad, in a large serving bowl, layer the field greens followed by the strawberries and candied pecans. Drizzle with the desired amount of vinaigrette. Toss and serve.

NIBBLES

These might be small bites but they pack in more flavor than the day is long! Southern snacks are full of personality and originality to say the least. If the Lump Crab Hushpuppies (page 122) aren't callin' your name, then try the Chile con Queso (page 132) or the Lemon Pepper Fried Okra (page 125).

Never had fried pickles and ranch dressing before? Maybe today is the day! And don't be surprised if this chapter of starters brings you to the finish line. Any way you slice it, these nibbles are sure to make happy bellies and smiling faces.

TEJAS JALAPEÑO POPPERS

(GRAIN-, DAIRY-, EGG-FREE)

This is the perfect party food with a hint of hot and a whole lotta yum! You might never guess
that these are dairy-free with their creamy filling, but they are. Topped with bacon,
these poppers will make the party people happier than pigs in slop!

YIELD: 4 SERVINGS

1 cup (150 g) cashews, macadamia nuts
or Brazil nuts, soaked for a minimum of
4 hours and drained

4 tsp (20 ml) apple cider vinegar

1 tsp (3 g) sea salt

½ tsp garlic powder

½ tsp onion powder

¼ tsp chili powder

¼ tsp cumin

½ cup (120 ml) flax milk (or other
dairy-free milk)

6 large jalapeño peppers, sliced in half
lengthwise and seeded

8 oz (227 g) bacon, cooked until crisp

Preheat the oven to 375°F (190°C, or gas mark 5).

Combine the nuts, apple cider vinegar, salt, garlic powder, onion powder, chili powder,
cumin and milk in a blender or food processor and puree until creamy. Spoon the filling
into the halved jalapeños, about 2 teaspoons (10 g) per half. Depending on the size of
your jalapeños, you may spoon slightly more or less filling.

Bake the filled peppers on a baking sheet for 15 minutes, then turn on the broiler and
allow to cook for an additional 3–4 minutes, being careful not to burn them. Remove
them from the oven and set aside to cool for a few minutes; while they do, chop up the
bacon, then sprinkle on top of the cooked peppers. You may have to press the bacon
pieces into the creamy filling to prevent them from sliding off. Serve warm or at
room temperature.

LUMP CRAB HUSHPUPPIES

(GRAIN-, DAIRY-, NIGHTSHADE-FREE)

Oh, sweet hushpuppies! If you are from the South, these were no doubt part of every seafood medley you ate. Whether spicy, savory or slightly sweet, hushpuppies are as native to Southern cuisine as they come. Add in lump crabmeat and you'll want to throw your hat over the windmill!

YIELD: 6 HUSHPUPPIES

Avocado oil, lard or coconut oil for frying

2 pastured eggs

¼ cup (30 g) almond flour

¼ cup (30 g) coconut flour

1 tbsp (15 ml) local raw honey

1 tsp (3 g) onion powder

¾ tsp sea salt

¼ cup (35 g) lump crabmeat

FOR SERVING

Homemade Tartar Sauce (page 44)

Heat the oil in large skillet over medium-high heat. While the oil is warming, combine all the other ingredients, except the tartar sauce, in a medium-size bowl, adding the crabmeat last. Make golf ball–size hushpuppies with the mixture and place in the heated oil. Fry each batch for approximately 5 minutes, turning them regularly, so they brown evenly on all sides. Try not to overcrowd your skillet as this can inhibit successful browning. Remove them with a slotted spoon and transfer carefully to a towel-lined plate. Serve while hot with Homemade Tartar Sauce.

LEMON PEPPER FRIED OKRA

(GRAIN-, DAIRY-, NUT-, NIGHTSHADE-FREE)

If you think you aren't a fan of okra, think again! This one has a perfect crispy coating and a lemon pepper kick. Paired with Ranch Dressing (page 131), it'll have you cookin' on the front burner!

YIELD: 4 SERVINGS

¼ cup (30 g) coconut flour

¼ cup (30 g) arrowroot flour

¼ cup (30 g) water chestnut flour

½ tsp freshly ground lemon pepper

½ tsp sea salt

¼ tsp garlic powder

1 egg

¼ cup (60 ml) flax milk (or preferred dairy-free milk)

Avocado oil, lard or coconut oil for frying

1 ½ cups (225 g) sliced okra (around 1" [2.5 cm] thick)

FOR SERVING

Ranch Dressing (page 131)

On a plate mix the flours, lemon pepper, salt and garlic powder until the seasonings are well combined. In a bowl, whisk the egg and flax milk together. This will help the crust adhere more successfully to the okra.

Heat the avocado oil in a medium-size skillet. You'll just need enough oil to coat the bottom of the skillet. Saturate the okra slices in the egg wash, and then dredge them in the flour mixture until they are all well coated.

Once the okra slices are generously coated in flour and the avocado oil begins to shimmer, gently place the okra into the hot oil. Fry the okra until nicely browned on all sides, turning them so that they do not burn. Once cooked, remove from the oil with a slotted spoon and place on clean towel-lined plate to remove excess oil. Serve hot with the ranch dressing as a quick appetizer or a crowd-pleasing side dish.

PALEO PIGGIES + HONEY MUSTARD

(GRAIN-, DAIRY-, NIGHTSHADE-FREE)

While it's true everything is bigger in Texas, these bite-size tidbits are always a party favorite amongst chitlins and grown-ups alike! Dunk 'em in this homemade honey mustard for even more to celebrate!

YIELD: 5 SERVINGS

FOR THE PALEO PIGGIES

1 ¼ cups (150 g) cashew flour (or cashew meal ground more finely)

2 tbsp (16 g) arrowroot flour

1 egg

1 tbsp (15 ml) olive oil

¼ tsp baking soda

¼ tsp sea salt

¼–½ tsp garlic powder

20–25 bite-size sausages, pastured when possible

FOR THE HONEY MUSTARD

¼ cup (60 ml) local raw honey

¼ cup (60 ml) organic yellow mustard

Preheat the oven to 375°F (190°C, or gas mark 5).

To make the piggies, in a bowl, combine all the ingredients except the sausages. The dough should not be too wet or sticky; you should be able to form a ball with ease. If it is still too wet, add a little more arrowroot flour, until you can form a ball to roll out. Roll out between two sheets of parchment paper to ¼ inch (6 mm) thick. Then, using a pizza cutter, cut triangles out of the dough, which will be rolled around the sausages.

Starting from the big side of a triangle, take one sausage and carefully roll it up until the dough is spiraled around. Take time in rolling them, as the dough is more fragile than a "glutenous" counterpart. Place on a baking sheet and bake for 10 minutes, or until the dough has crisped up; they will not become as golden as some other versions.

To make the honey mustard, simply combine the honey and yellow mustard and stir well! Grab your piggies and get to dippin'!

CANTINA TORTILLA CHIPS + HOMEMADE SALSA

(GRAIN-, EGG-, DAIRY-, NUT-FREE)

Fresh salsa takes the cake, er, um, chip, over any of the bottled stuff. Once you see how quick and simple it is to make your own, you will never want store-bought again. Paired with grain-free crispy tortilla chips, this snack will make you feel like anything is possible with real food!

YIELD: 3 SERVINGS

FOR THE SALSA

1 cup (180 g) diced tomatoes

½ cup (130 g) organic tomato sauce (jarred)

1 cup (60 g) chopped cilantro

1 small red onion, diced

1 jalapeño, seeded and minced

1 tsp (3 g) (or 2 cloves) minced garlic

Juice from 2 limes

¼ tsp sea salt

¼ tsp cracked black pepper

FOR SERVING

Tortilla Chips (page 187) or store-bought sweet potato chips

To make the salsa, it doesn't get much easier than this: simply combine all the ingredients, chill and serve with the chips!

CHIPOTLE STUFFED MUSHROOMS

(GRAIN-, DAIRY-, NUT-FREE)

Stuffed mushrooms are a favorite for small bites. These kick it up with chipotle mayonnaise baked right in for a zesty, tender filling with a little pep that will keep you on your toes!

YIELD: 10 SERVINGS

2 lbs (908 g) whole white mushrooms, cleaned and stemmed

1 medium onion, diced

1 lb (454 g) pastured breakfast sausage (or best quality available)

1 cup (240 ml) homemade mayonnaise (or high-quality store-bought)

1 chipotle pepper in adobo sauce, minced

½ tsp adobo sauce, check for ingredient quality

Preheat the oven to 375°F (190°C, or gas mark 5).

Place the stemmed mushrooms on a foil-lined baking sheet. In a large skillet, sauté the onion and sausage over high heat until the sausage is cooked through, about 8 minutes.

While the sausage is cooking, puree the mayonnaise, chipotle pepper and adobo sauce in a blender or food processor. Once the sausage is cooked through, remove from the heat and stir in the chipotle mayo. Spoon the filling into the mushroom caps, being careful not to overfill. Bake for 20–25 minutes, or until the stuffing starts to brown nicely along with the mushrooms.

DEEP SOUTH FRIED PICKLES

(GRAIN-, DAIRY-, NUT-, NIGHTSHADE-FREE)

While I am not sure if there was an actual prize awarded for whoever came up with this concept, there certainly should have been! Instead of bleached white flour, these use water chestnut flour, which is not only grain free but nut free as well.

YIELD: 2 SERVINGS

FOR THE FRIED PICKLES

1 egg

¼ cup (60 ml) flax milk (or other dairy-free milk)

½ cup (60 g) water chestnut flour

¼ tsp freshly cracked black pepper

⅓ tsp sea salt

¼ tsp garlic powder

Avocado oil (or preferred cooking fat) for frying

1 ½ cups (225 g) high-quality dill pickle slices

FOR THE RANCH DRESSING

⅓ cup (75 ml) homemade mayo (or high quality store-bought)

¼ cup (60 ml) flax milk (or other dairy-free milk)

1 tsp (5g) fresh dill, minced

1 tsp (5g) fresh chives, minced

¼ tsp sea salt

¼ tsp black pepper

¼ tsp garlic powder

¼ tsp onion powder

¼ tsp dried parsley

Juice from ½ small lemon

In a bowl, whisk together the egg and flax milk. On a plate, combine the water chestnut flour and seasonings.

Heat enough avocado oil to line the bottom of a medium-size skillet over high heat. Soak the pickle slices in the egg wash and then dredge them on both sides in the flour mixture.

For an extra crispy coating, soak them again and dredge for a second time. In small batches fry the pickle slices for about 3 minutes per side, or until crispy. Some may be more golden brown than others, so you do not need to rely on color to indicate crispness. Using a slotted spoon, remove the pickles from the hot oil and lay them pon a towel-lined plate to absorb excess oil. Jazz it up by serving with Ranch Dressing. To make, mix all ingredients in a bowl until combined.

CHILE CON QUESO + GRAIN-FREE TORTILLAS

(GRAIN-, EGG-, DAIRY-FREE)

In the majority of the Southern states, queso doesn't simply mean "cheese;" it is reflective of the very stuff that sustains life. Ask any devoted Tex-Mex fan and she'll sing the same campfire song! This dairy-free version is so shockingly cheesy, even the aficionados may be fooled.

YIELD: 4 SERVINGS

FOR THE CHILE CON QUESO

1 cup (150 g) cashews, soaked for at least 4 hours and drained

¼ tsp garlic powder

¼ tsp onion powder

¼ tsp paprika

½ tsp sea salt

¼ cup (25 g) jarred pimentos, drained

½ cup (120 ml) water

¼ cup (60 g) Homemade Salsa (page 128)

Chopped fresh cilantro (optional)

FOR SERVING

4 large or 8 small Tortillas (page 189) or store-bought sweet potato chips

To make the chile con queso, combine the drained cashews, seasonings, pimentos and water in a blender or food processor. Blend until creamy. Empty the contents into a small saucepan and heat over medium heat for 5 minutes, stirring regularly to prevent burning. Remove from the heat and add in the salsa and cilantro, if desired. Serve with the warm tortillas for dipping.

GUACAMOLE TOSTADAS

(GRAIN-, DAIRY-, NUT-, EGG-FREE)

When you combine this crispy tostada with the creamy avocado and the fresh ripe tomatoes
of the guacamole, you will begin to wonder if ever there had been a more perfect combination.
What's more is this tostada is grain, nut and egg free!

YIELD: 6 SERVINGS

FOR THE GUACAMOLE

2 medium-size avocados, peeled and pitted

½ small onion, diced

Handful chopped cilantro

Juice of 1 lime

1 vine-ripened tomato, diced

1 jalapeño, diced + seeded (optional)

½ tsp garlic sea salt

½ tsp onion powder

¼ tsp freshly cracked black pepper

FOR SERVING

6 Tostadas (page 188) or store-bought sweet potato chips

To make the guacamole, combine the avocado flesh, onion, cilantro, lime juice, tomato, jalapeño, garlic sea salt, onion powder and black pepper. Coarsely mash these ingredients, being careful not to overmix. Serve by spreading a tablespoon (15 g) on a tostada or chill for later. If you don't plan to eat it right away, place the avocado pit in the guacamole to help keep it from browning in the fridge. Keep it chilled and covered until ready to use.

CAJUN-SPICED CHICKEN WINGS

(GRAIN-, DAIRY-, NUT-FREE)

You'll wanna make sure you're wearin' your grown-up britches for this one! These Cajun-seasoned wings will put a fire under your saddle and a smile on your face.

YIELD: 4 SERVINGS

3 tbsp (45 ml) homemade mayonnaise (or high-quality store-bought)

3 tbsp (45 ml) olive oil

½ cup (120 ml) dairy-free hot wing sauce

2 lbs (908 g) pastured chicken wings and/or drumettes

½ cup (60 g) tapioca starch

½ tsp sea salt

½ tsp oregano

½ tsp thyme

½ tsp cayenne

¼ tsp white pepper

½ tsp onion powder

½ tsp garlic powder

½ tsp paprika

FOR SERVING

Ranch Dressing (page 131)

Preheat the oven to 400°F (200°C, or gas mark 6).

In a large zip-top bag, combine the mayonnaise, olive oil and hot wing sauce. Shake to combine. Add the chicken wings and shake to coat evenly. Sprinkle in the tapioca starch and shake again until all the wings are coated in flour. If you prefer, you may use a large stainless steel or glass mixing bowl. Place the wings out on a foil-lined baking sheet.

In a small bowl, mix together all of the remaining seasonings. Sprinkle the mixture over the wings, as generously or as sparingly as desired. The more seasoning sprinkled, the more kick the wings will have. It is not necessary to use all of the seasoning. Bake for 40-45 minutes or until crispy. Carefully remove from oven and serve with dairy-free ranch dressing!

FRESHLY BAKED + SWEETIE PIES

If you've ever set foot in a traditional Southern kitchen, you've probably been greeted with a big pitcher of tea or lemonade and somethin' freshly baked right out of the oven. Southerners don't take their breads or pies lightly, so you can bet this chapter is baked from the heart, and without grain to boot!

In this section you'll find Deep South favorites like Tres Leches Cake (page 169), "Corny" Bread Muffins (page 139), Grain-Free Chocolate Zucchini Bread (page 148) and Chocolate Chip Georgia Pecan Pie (page 155). And of course, a Nut-Free Biscuit (page 141) to sop up that extra gravy! If you ever worried about having to sacrifice your favorites when going grain free, this chapter is for you!

"CORNY" BREAD MUFFINS + HONEY BUTTER

(GRAIN-, DAIRY-, SOY-, NIGHTSHADE-FREE)

Well, making cornbread without corn is kinda tricky, but since corn is indeed a grain, "real" cornbread will not be found here. As any good Southerner knows, the honey sure helps make a good cornbread, and that, my friends, is baked right into these tasty lil' replicas!

YIELD: 12 MUFFINS

FOR THE HONEY BUTTER

2 tbsp (30 ml) full-fat coconut milk

3 tbsp (45 ml) olive oil

2 tbsp (30 ml) coconut oil, melted

3 tbsp (45 ml) avocado oil

½ tsp sea salt

2–3 tbsp (30–45 ml) local raw honey, to taste

FOR THE MUFFINS

1 cup (120 g) blanched almond flour

3 tbsp (24 g) coconut flour

2 tsp (6 g) baking soda

4 eggs

½ cup (120 ml) palm shortening

3 tbsp (45 ml) local raw honey

3 tbsp (45 ml) pure applesauce (nothing added)

1 tsp (5 ml) apple cider vinegar

To make the honey butter, whisk all the ingredients together vigorously in a small mixing bowl for a minute or two. Pour into a freezer-safe bowl and place in the freezer for 30 minutes.

Preheat the oven to 350°F (180°C, or gas mark 4). Prepare a muffin tin with paper liners.

To make the muffins, combine the flours and baking soda in one bowl and then combine the eggs, shortening, honey, applesauce and vinegar in another. Incorporate the wet ingredients into the dry, using a hand mixer if necessary to ensure the mixture is combined well. Pour the batter into the muffin cups, filling each around three-fourths full. Bake for 15–20 minutes, or until a toothpick inserted into the center comes out clean.

Once the butter has been frozen for 30 minutes, remove from the freezer and mash with a fork to soften. If the butter and honey have separated slightly, that is normal. Using the fork, stir until the butter is creamy and spreadable. Serve right away with the muffins, then refrigerate the butter for later use.

PECAN PIE MUFFINS +
SPICED CANDIED PECAN TOPPING

(GRAIN-, DAIRY-, SOY-, NIGHTSHADE-FREE)

When eating a whole pie just seems like a bit much, mosey on over to this here pecan pie muffin recipe.
It will satisfy that craving in a slightly more understated fashion!

YIELD: 12 MUFFINS

FOR THE MUFFINS

4 organic pastured eggs

⅓ cup (80 ml) coconut oil, melted

1 tbsp (8 g) coconut flour

1 ¼ cups (188 g) pecan halves or pieces

⅓ cup (80 ml) pure maple syrup

⅛ tsp sea salt

1 tsp (3 g) baking soda

FOR THE SPICED CANDIED PECAN TOPPING

½ cup (75 g) pecan pieces

2 tbsp (30 ml) honey

¼ tsp ground cinnamon

Pinch of ground nutmeg

Pinch of ground cloves

Preheat the oven to 350°F (180°C, or gas mark 4). Prepare a muffin tin with paper liners.

To make the muffins, combine all the ingredients in a blender and blend until creamy. Fill the muffin cups half to two-thirds full and bake for 20 minutes, or until a toothpick inserted into the center comes out clean.

To make the spiced candied pecans, line a small baking sheet with a piece of parchment paper. In a bowl, mix together the pecan pieces, honey and spices. Once the nuts are coated well, spread them out on the prepared baking sheet and bake for 10 minutes. Remove from the oven and divide the topping over the muffins. Serve warm.

NUT-FREE BISCUITS + DAIRY-FREE BUTTER

(GRAIN-, DAIRY-, NUT-, SOY-, NIGHTSHADE-, EGG-FREE)

If you want to try a different biscuit than the recipe listed in "When the Rooster Crows" (page 28), or you can't tolerate nuts, this is the perfect option. These are baked up in less than 30 minutes and served with homemade dairy-free butter. Want a little extra drizzle of honey? Go for it, I won't tell!

YIELD: 6 BISCUITS

FOR THE BISCUITS

½ cup (60 g) coconut flour

¼ cup (60 ml) palm shortening, melted

1 tbsp (15 ml) honey

¼ cup (30 g) potato starch

½ tsp baking soda

Pinch of salt

½–¾ cup (120–180 ml) full-fat coconut milk

FOR THE DAIRY-FREE BUTTER

2 tbsp (30 ml) full-fat coconut milk

3 tbsp (45 ml) olive oil

2 tbsp (30 ml) coconut oil, melted

3 tbsp (45 ml) avocado oil

½ tsp salt

Preheat the oven to 350°F (180°C, or gas mark 4).

To make the biscuits, place all the biscuit ingredients in a mixing bowl and stir to combine. Start by using only ½ cup (120 ml) of coconut milk and adding more as needed. The dough should be thick and stiff, not like batter. Once the desired consistency is reached, spoon 6 equal-size heaps of dough onto a parchment-lined baking sheet. Bake for 15 minutes, watching carefully so that they do not burn. Remove from the oven and let cool slightly.

To make the butter, combine all the ingredients in a blender and blend until creamy. Pour the mixture into a glass dish with a lid and freeze for 30 minutes (or refrigerate until solidified). Spread the butter on a warm biscuit to your heart's content. Store any unused butter in the refrigerator.

MINI DINNER ROLLS + GRAPE JELLY

(GRAIN-, DAIRY-, NUT-, SOY-, NIGHTSHADE-FREE)

Everyone in the South knows you need a proper bread for soppin' up the extra gravy! Be it a biscuit or a dinner roll, it's a necessity of the utmost importance. These lil' bites of love are grain and nut free, making them a perfect option for those with multiple sensitivities. Paired with this simple grape jelly, you'll never feel deprived of bread and spread again!

YIELD: 10 ROLLS

FOR THE GRAPE JELLY

2–3 tsp (6–8 g) grass-fed gelatin

1 cup (235 ml) organic grape juice

Squeeze of lemon (optional)

FOR THE DINNER ROLLS

1 ½ cups (270 g) peeled and coarsely chopped yuca

1 tbsp (15 ml) avocado oil, coconut oil, lard or olive oil

2 pastured eggs

½ tsp garlic sea salt

1 tsp (5 ml) apple cider vinegar

½ tsp baking soda

1 tbsp (12 g) coconut palm sugar

To make the jelly, quickly stir the gelatin powder into the grape juice in a small saucepan until it dissolves completely. Place over high heat and cook for about 2 minutes. Remove from the heat, squeeze in the lemon juice, if desired, and stir. Transfer to a glass bowl (preferably with a lid) and refrigerate until it starts to congeal, about 20-30 minutes. Stir again and use once the desired consistency is achieved.

Preheat the oven to 375°F (190°C, or gas mark 5). Grease the cups of a muffin tin.

To make the rolls, fill a stockpot with water and bring to a boil over high heat. Add the yuca and boil for 20–25 minutes, or until fork-tender. Drain the water and remove the yuca from the pot. Remove the woody core once the yuca is cool enough to handle.

In a high-powered blender or food processor (preferably with a tamper), blend the yuca and oil until a dough forms. Add the eggs, salt, vinegar, baking soda and sugar and blend until the batter is creamy and without lumps. Spoon the batter into the muffin cups, about 1 tablespoon (15 g) per roll. Bake for 20 minutes, or until a toothpick inserted into the center comes out clean. Serve warm with just about any main course and a smear of jelly for a touch of sweet!

PALEO BANANA BREAD

(GRAIN-, DAIRY-, NUT-, SOY-, NIGHTSHADE-FREE)

A warm slice of banana bread practically screams home cookin' down South. This recipe is enough to impress the pickiest banana bread connoisseur, despite its twist on the traditional ingredients!

YIELD: 8 SERVINGS

2 bananas

4 eggs

½ cup (60 g) arrowroot flour

2 tbsp (16 g) coconut flour

3 tbsp (45 ml) local raw honey

1 tsp (5 ml) pure vanilla extract

¼ cup (60 ml) olive oil or preferred cooking fat

1 tsp (3 g) baking soda

¼ tsp sea salt

½ cup (75 g) walnut or pecan pieces (optional)

Preheat the oven to 350°F (180°C, or gas mark 4).

In a blender, combine all the ingredients except the nuts, if using, and puree. Pour the batter into a greased loaf pan (glass is preferred) and spread evenly. If you choose to incorporate nuts, you may sprinkle them over the top of the unbaked loaf at this time; this of course negates the "nut-free" option. Some of the nuts will sink into the batter and some will rest on top. Bake for 35–45 minutes, or until a toothpick inserted into the center comes out clean.

CHEF'S TIP: Paleo bread loaves do not rise as much as their glutenous counterparts. Using a smaller loaf pan will help create more "lift" in your loaf.

SWEET POTATO SLIDER BUNS

(GRAIN-, DAIRY-, NUT-, SOY-, NIGHTSHADE-FREE)

These mini slider buns can sandwich just about any savory filling. Chicken salad, pulled pork or lil' grass-fed burgers, they can make a snack or a full meal. I'd say that makes these sweeter than stolen honey!

YIELD: 8 BUNS

3 pastured eggs

¼ cup (30 g) sweet potato flour

¼ cup (30 g) arrowroot flour

1 tbsp (8 g) coconut flour

½ tsp sea salt

1 tbsp (12 g) coconut palm sugar or maple sugar

2 tbsp (30 ml) avocado oil or preferred cooking fat

½ tsp baking soda

Preheat the oven to 375°F (190°C, or gas mark 5). Grease a muffin tin.

Combine all the ingredients in a blender until smooth. Pour the batter into 8 cups in the muffin tin, about half to two-thirds full. Bake for 20 minutes and remove promptly from oven. They should pop out of the muffin tin with ease. Slice them horizontally to use as slider buns.

GRAIN-FREE APPLE CRISP

(GRAIN-, DAIRY-, EGG-, SOY-, NIGHTSHADE-FREE)

A good, homemade apple crisp can transport you back to your childhood with a single bite, y'all. Instead of oats or flour, this recipe uses a combination of pecans, coconut and pumpkin seeds to deliver a delicious taste of home!

YIELD: 6 SERVINGS

5 small apples, diced (about 4 cups [600 g])

3 tbsp (45 ml) pure maple syrup

5 tbsp (60 g) coconut palm sugar, divided

⅓ cup (50 g) pecans

⅓ cup (25 g) unsweetened shredded coconut

⅓ cup (40 g) coconut flour

⅓ cup (50 g) pumpkin seeds

⅛ tsp sea salt

⅓ cup (80 ml) coconut oil, melted

FOR SERVING

Coconut Whipped Cream (page 159, optional)

Preheat the oven to 375°F (190°C, or gas mark 5).

Place the diced apples in a small greased casserole dish (8 x 8 inches [20 x 20 cm] works well). Drizzle the maple syrup and 3 tablespoons (36 g) of the coconut sugar over the apples.

In a blender or food processor, gently pulse the pecans, shredded coconut, coconut flour, pumpkin seeds, salt and remaining 2 tablespoons (24 g) coconut sugar. Once the mixture is "crumbly" and coarse, sprinkle it over the apples. Last, drizzle the coconut oil over the coconut and nut mixture and then bake for 30 minutes, until the topping is crispy and the apples are bubbly. Remove and allow to cool only slightly, then serve warm. Top with Coconut Whipped Cream, if desired, for an extra treat.

GRAIN-FREE
CHOCOLATE ZUCCHINI BREAD

(GRAIN-, DAIRY-, NUT-, SOY-, NIGHTSHADE-FREE)

This bread is so authentic you'd never guess the grain was missing! Served warm out of the oven or toasted the next day, it is a crowd-pleaser anytime and a perfect way to use up your summer's harvest.

YIELD: 8 SERVINGS

4 pastured eggs

1 banana

2 tbsp (16 g) cocoa powder

¼ cup (60 ml) pure maple syrup

½ cup (60 g) coconut flour

1 tsp (3 g) baking soda

1 tbsp (15 ml) coconut oil, melted

¼ tsp sea salt

1 tsp (3 g) ground cinnamon

¼ tsp ground nutmeg

1 medium zucchini, shredded

½ cup (90 g) dairy-free chocolate chips (optional)

Preheat the oven to 350°F (180°C, or gas mark 4).

In a blender, combine all the ingredients except the shredded zucchini. Blend until well combined and then pour the batter into a mixing bowl. The batter will thicken slightly over the next few minutes. Fold in the shredded zucchini and chocolate chips (if using) and stir well. Pour the mixture into a greased loaf pan (glass is preferred) and bake for about an hour, or until a toothpick inserted into the center comes out clean. Let cool, then gently pry it away from the sides of the pan and invert onto a plate. Invert again. Slice and serve warm.

CHEF'S TIP: Paleo bread loaves rise less than traditional ones. Using a smaller loaf pan will yield a taller loaf.

MIXED BERRY COBBLER

(GRAIN-, DAIRY-, NUT-, EGG-, SOY-, NIGHTSHADE-FREE)

There is no such thing as a list of Southern desserts if cobbler isn't one of them. Be it apple, peach or berry, cobbler is always a winner! This berry version is so scrumptious, you'd never know the crumbly, toasty topping was made with only a handful of healthy whole foods.

YIELD: 6 SERVINGS

FOR THE TOPPING

¼ cup (30 g) coconut flour

¼ cup (20 g) unsweetened shredded coconut

¼ cup (30 g) sweet potato flour

1 tbsp (12 g) coconut palm sugar

⅓ cup (80 ml) coconut oil, melted, or preferred cooking fat

Pinch of salt

FOR THE COBBLER

1 ½ lbs (680 g) mixed berries (strawberries, blueberries, raspberries, blackberries)

¼ cup (50 g) coconut palm sugar

Zest from 1 clementine or tangerine

FOR SERVING

Coconut Whipped Cream (page 159, optional)

Preheat the oven to 350°F (180°C, or gas mark 4).

To make the topping, in a bowl, combine the topping ingredients and set aside.

To make the cobbler, rinse and trim the berries as necessary. Add the sugar and zest and toss gently to combine. Transfer to a small, greased casserole dish, then sprinkle on the topping mixture. Bake for 25–30 minutes, or until the topping is crunchy but not burned. Remove from the oven and serve warm, topped with the Coconut Whipped Cream, if desired, for extra yums!

COCONUT CUSTARD PIE

(GRAIN-, DAIRY-, SOY-, NIGHTSHADE-FREE)

Growing up I remember a BBQ joint smack dab in the middle of nowhere that folks traveled for hours to visit.
In addition to its famous smoked meats, the pies kept people coming back for more year after year.
This coconut custard pie is my best recreation of that childhood favorite!

YIELD: 8 SERVINGS

FOR THE CRUST

½ cup (60 g) coconut flour

½ cup (60 g) pecan flour

¼ tsp salt

¼ tsp baking soda

1 tsp (3 g) ground cinnamon

¼ cup (60 ml) honey

¼ cup (60 ml) coconut oil, melted

1 egg

1 tsp (5 ml) pure vanilla extract

FOR THE CUSTARD

4 pastured eggs

3 tbsp (45 ml) pure maple syrup

½ tsp pure vanilla extract

¼ tsp sea salt

1 (13.5 oz [378 g]) can full-fat organic coconut milk, divided

1 ½ tbsp (12 g) tapioca flour

¼ cup (20 g) unsweetened shredded coconut

FOR SERVING

Coconut Whipped Cream (page 159, optional)

Preheat the oven to 350°F (180°C, or gas mark 4).

To make the crust, combine all the crust ingredients in a mixing bowl. Lightly grease pie tin and press the mixture into a nice even layer in the base and up the sides. Par-bake the crust for 5 minutes, remove and freeze for 20 minutes while you make the filling.

To make the filling, combine the eggs, maple syrup, vanilla and salt in a bowl and whisk well to combine. In a small saucepan over medium heat, whisk together ¼ cup (60 ml) of the coconut milk and the tapioca flour until there are no lumps. Add the remaining coconut milk and whisk over medium heat for about 5–8 minutes, or until it begins to thicken. Remove from the heat and very slowly begin to incorporate into the egg mixture, whisking continuously so as not to cook the eggs.

Remove the pie shell from the freezer and pour in the filling. Bake for 15 minutes, remove and evenly sprinkle the shredded coconut on top of the pie. Return to the oven for another 10–15 minutes or until the center is cooked through. Chill or serve warm, depending on your preference. Top with Coconut Whipped Cream, if desired.

CHOCOLATE CHIP GEORGIA PECAN PIE

(GRAIN-, DAIRY-, SOY-, NIGHTSHADE-FREE)

Oh my pie! I can't be certain, but I think there is a Southern law that says you must eat your weight in pie if ever in the Southern states. Pie is not just dessert—it is as essential as the air you breathe. This version is the perfect marriage between traditional pecan pie and chocolate!

YIELD: 8 SERVINGS

FOR THE CRUST

1 cup (120 g) cashew meal (or grind your own)

1 cup (120 g) almond flour

1 egg

1 tbsp (15 ml) pure maple syrup

¼ cup (30 g) tapioca flour

Pinch of salt

FOR THE FILLING

3 eggs

3 tbsp (45 ml) coconut oil, melted

¾ cup (130 g) dairy- and soy-free chocolate chips, plus more for sprinkling on top (optional)

1 ½ cups (225 g) pecan halves

¼ tsp sea salt

½ cup (100 g) maple sugar

1 tsp (5 ml) pure vanilla extract

FOR SERVING

Coconut Whipped Cream (page 159, optional)

Preheat the oven to 350°F (180°C, or gas mark 4).

To make the crust, combine all the ingredients in a bowl and mix until well incorporated. Lightly grease pie tin and press the mixture into a nice even layer in the base and up the sides. Par-bake the crust for 5 minutes, then remove from the oven.

To make the filling, mix all the ingredients in a bowl until well combined, and then pour into the par-baked pie shell. If adding more chocolate chips, sprinkle them on top. Return the filled pie to the oven and bake for 30–40 minutes, or until set. Remove from the oven and set aside to cool slightly. Serve warm with a dollop of Coconut Whipped Cream, if desired.

BOURBON STREET BREAD PUDDING + CARAMEL SAUCE

(GRAIN-, DAIRY-, SOY-FREE)

If you've been to Louisiana, you've likely tried the beignets and the bread pudding.
It might be illegal not to indulge in these two, actually. This grain-free version features raisins,
nuts and a caramel sauce for a slightly addictive Southern delight.

YIELD: 6 SERVINGS

FOR THE BREAD

½ cup (60 g) potato starch

½ cup (60 g) tapioca starch

¼ cup (30 g) water chestnut flour

⅓ cup (80 ml) local raw honey or pure maple syrup

6 pastured eggs

3 tbsp (45 ml) coconut oil, melted, or preferred cooking fat

3 tbsp (24 g) flax seeds

1 tsp (3 g) baking soda

1 tbsp (15 ml) apple cider vinegar

½ tsp ground cinnamon

½ tsp ground nutmeg

FOR THE PUDDING MIXTURE

3 pastured eggs

1 ½ cups (355 ml) full-fat coconut milk

1 tsp (5 ml) pure vanilla extract

½ cup (75 g) pecan or walnut pieces

½ cup (75 g) organic raisins

FOR THE CARAMEL SAUCE

½ cup (120 ml) full-fat coconut milk

¼ cup (50 g) coconut palm sugar

Preheat the oven to 350°F (180°C, or gas mark 4).

To make the bread, combine all of the ingredients in a blender and blend until pureed. Pour into a small greased casserole dish or loaf pan and bake for 40 minutes, or until a toothpick inserted into the center comes out clean. Remove from the oven, remove from the casserole dish and slice into cubes. Place the cubes on a baking sheet and return it to the oven for 20 minutes, or until toasted.

To make the pudding mixture, whisk together the eggs, coconut milk, vanilla, nuts and raisins in a bowl. Once the cubed bread is toasted, remove it from the oven and place it back into the casserole dish. Pour the milk and egg mixture over the top and stir to coat. Place the casserole dish back into the oven and bake for a final 25 minutes.

To make the caramel sauce, combine the ingredients in a small saucepan over high heat and bring to a boil. Allow to boil for about 15 minutes, or until the mixture thickens and reduces to a thick caramel syrup. Remove the baked bread pudding from the oven, drizzle with the caramel sauce and serve warm.

EMERALD COAST KEY LIME PIE + COCONUT WHIPPED CREAM

(GRAIN-, DAIRY-, EGG-, SOY-, NIGHTSHADE-FREE)

Growing up, my family would make their annual trek to the Florida Panhandle, where I'd watch my mom and grandma enthusiastically order their Key lime pie. I have such fond memories of those trips and had to recreate this favorite in honor of that tradition.

YIELD: 8 SERVINGS

FOR THE CRUST

½ cup (75 g) pecan pieces

½ cup (75 g) dried mulberries

½ cup (60 g) coconut flour

¼ tsp sea salt

6 tbsp (90 ml) coconut oil melted

FOR THE FILLING

1 (13.5 oz [378 g]) can full-fat coconut milk, divided

½ cup + 1 tbsp (135 ml) Key lime juice

5 tbsp (75 ml) local raw honey

1 tsp (3 g) Key lime zest

1 tbsp (8 g) grass-fed gelatin

FOR THE COCONUT WHIPPED CREAM

1 (13.5 oz [378 g]) can full-fat coconut milk, refrigerated for at least 2 hours (preferably overnight)

5 drops liquid stevia extract or 1 tbsp (12 g) coconut palm sugar

To make the crust, pulse the pecan pieces and dried mulberries in a food processor or blender until a fine-grained texture is achieved. Add in the coconut flour and sea salt and pulse once again, briefly. Empty the contents into a mixing bowl and drizzle in the coconut oil, distributing it evenly. Work the oil through the mixture with your hands, then press the mixture into the bottom and up the sides of a pie tin (use the back of a spoon if the crust sticks to your fingers). The crust should cover the bottom of the tin and about halfway up the sides; pressing it too thin could potentially cause it to crack when serving, so take care when distributing. Freeze the crust for about 20 minutes while preparing the filling.

To make the filling, combine all but 2 tablespoons (30 ml) of the coconut milk, the lime juice, honey and zest in a small saucepan. Place the reserved coconut milk in a small bowl. Heat the mixture over medium heat, stirring, until warm. Add the gelatin to the reserved coconut milk, whisking until well combined. Add the gelatin mixture to the saucepan, stirring continuously for about a minute.

Remove the pie tin from the freezer and pour the filling into the hardened crust. Place the pie back into the freezer for about 45 minutes for it to set. You can alternatively place it in the refrigerator, though it can easily take twice as long to set this way.

To make the whipped cream, combine the cream, skimmed off the top of the coconut milk, with the stevia. Avoid using the watery part of the coconut milk, which separates out upon refrigeration, because it will prevent the cream from becoming as sturdy when whipped. If you choose to use the coconut sugar, please note that it can tint the whipped cream ever so slightly; the liquid stevia is clear and will keep the whipped cream white. This is only a cosmetic variation as both versions taste similarly. Use an immersion blender or hand mixer to whip the cream until it has a whipped cream consistency, about 2 minutes.

Slice and serve, keeping pie and whipped cream chilled when not plating.

PALEO BLONDIES

(GRAIN-, DAIRY-, NUT-, SOY-FREE)

Blondies are usually packed with butter, sugar and bleached white flour, which makes them clearly off-limits for a grain-free lifestyle. This tasty rendition luckily still creates that moist, buttery appeal but uses only high-quality ingredients. If that ain't bright like a new penny, I dunno what is!

YIELD: 16 SERVINGS

¼ cup (50 g) coconut palm sugar

¼ cup (60 ml) full-fat coconut milk

½ cup (60 g) arrowroot flour

½ cup (60 g) potato starch

2 eggs

3 tbsp (45 ml) coconut oil, melted

3 tbsp (45 ml) shortening

1 tsp (5 ml) pure vanilla extract

1 tsp (3 g) baking soda

¼ tsp sea salt

¾ cup (130 g) dairy- and soy-free chocolate chips

Preheat the oven to 350°F (180°C, or gas mark 4).

In a small saucepan, heat the coconut palm sugar and coconut milk over high heat, stirring regularly, for about 5 minutes. Look for the mixture to thicken, darken and reduce by about half. Once it becomes more caramel-like, remove from the heat and set aside.

Meanwhile in a mixing bowl, place all the remaining ingredients except for the chocolate chips and stir until well combined. Pour in the caramel and then the chocolate chips. Pour the mixture into a small greased casserole dish (8 x 8 inches [20 x 20 cm] works well). These do not rise that much, so using a larger casserole dish will yield a flatter blondie. Bake for 20 minutes, or until a toothpick inserted into the center comes out clean. Remove from the oven and allow to cool for about 5 minutes before slicing.

RODEO FUNNEL CAKES

(GRAIN-, DAIRY-, NUT-, SOY-, NIGHTSHADE-FREE)

If you've ever been to a Texas rodeo, then you will have walked away with a set of memories to last a lifetime. From the world's best country music singers, to the livestock show, to the boots and hats, one memory will never escape you—the funnel cakes. You can smell them from a mile away, and this one hits as close to home as the original, but kicks the white flour and sugar to the curb. Trust me, you won't miss the originals with this sassy imposter!

YIELD: 6 FUNNEL CAKES

FOR THE FUNNEL CAKE

Coconut oil or avocado oil for frying

1 cup (120 g) tapioca flour

2 pastured eggs

2 tbsp (30 ml) pure maple syrup

2 tbsp (30 ml) avocado oil

Pinch of salt

FOR THE "POWDERED SUGAR" SPRINKLE

1 tbsp (12 g) maple sugar or coconut palm sugar

3 tbsp (24 g) tapioca flour

To make the funnel cakes, pour the oil into a saucepan to a depth of 1 inch (2.5 cm) and heat over medium-high heat (using a small saucepan will help conserve how much oil you pour in). Combine the tapioca flour, eggs, syrup, avocado oil and salt in a bowl. Stir until the batter is well combined.

Spoon the batter into a pastry bag and once the oil is shimmering (hot enough to fry in), quickly drizzle the batter into the hot oil, overlapping and making sure to not concentrate on one area (you are basically making squiggles and curlicues as you drizzle). Allow the underside to brown, around 1 minute, then use a flat slotted spoon to flip the funnel cake over and brown the other side. Remove the funnel cake from the oil and place on a towel-lined plate.

To make the sprinkle, combine the maple sugar and tapioca flour in a small bowl. Using a sifter, shake the sugar mixture on top of the funnel cake. Serve hot!

CHURRO DOUGHNUT HOLES

(GRAIN-, DAIRY-, NUT-, SOY-, NIGHTSHADE-FREE)

These crispy fried doughnuts are beyond popular in many border towns in Texas. Though typically piped as a starburst shape into hot oil, this recipe captures the essence of the churro but takes out a little of the leg work, leaving more time to eat them!

YIELD: 5 SERVINGS

---

2 cups (360 g) peeled and coarsely chopped yuca root

¾ cup (150 g) coconut palm sugar, divided

1 tbsp (15 ml) avocado oil, plus more for frying

3 eggs

½ cup (100 g) coconut flour

½ tsp baking soda

1 tbsp (8 g) ground cinnamon

Pinch of ground nutmeg

Fill a large stockpot with water and bring to a boil over high heat. Add the yuca and boil for 20–25 minutes, or until fork-tender. Drain and allow to cool slightly. Remove the woody core from the center of each root once cool enough to handle.

In a heavy-duty blender, combine the yuca, ½ cup (100 g) of the coconut palm sugar, 1 tablespoon (15 ml) avocado oil, eggs, coconut flour and baking soda. Blend until thoroughly combined. Transfer the dough to a mixing bowl.

Heat about ½ inch (1.3 cm) avocado oil in a small saucepan over high heat. By using a smaller saucepan, you can use less oil and have the doughnut holes fry more evenly.

Take 1 tablespoon (15 g) of dough at a time and roll into a ball. Place in the oil and fry until golden brown, about 2-4 minutes, using a spoon to rotate the balls of dough so that all sides are evenly browned. Repeat until all the dough is used, frying in small batches so as not to overcrowd the pan. Using a slotted spoon, remove from the hot oil and set on a towel-lined plate.

In a small bowl, combine the remaining ¼ cup (50 g) coconut palm sugar, cinnamon and nutmeg. One at a time, roll the doughnut holes in the cinnamon sugar mixture, until all sides are coated. Serve warm.

SOPAPILLAS

(GRAIN-, DAIRY-, NUT-, EGG-, SOY-, NIGHTSHADE-FREE)

As a young girl, I remember awaiting dessert with such anticipation when we would dine out at Tex-Mex restaurants. We'd order a giant basket of sopapillas either drizzled with honey or dusted with powdered sugar. Either way they came out, this hot fried dough was the best finale!

YIELD: 16 SERVINGS

---

2 lbs (908 g) peeled and coarsely chopped yuca root

½ cup (100 g) coconut sugar

¼ tsp sea salt

3 tbsp (45 ml) coconut oil, melted

Coconut oil or avocado oil for frying

FOR SERVING

Powdered stevia, tapioca starch or honey

Fill a stockpot with water and bring to a boil over high heat. Add the yuca and boil for 20–25 minutes, or until fork-tender. Drain the water and remove the yuca from the pot. Remove the woody core once the yuca is cool enough to handle.

Add the yuca, coconut sugar, sea salt and 3 tablespoons (45 ml) oil to a heavy-duty blender or food processor. If using a blender with a tamper, start on low speed and vigorously use the tamper to push the yuca chunks under the blades. Slowly increase the speed until the yuca has been blended into a dough. Using the tamper will ensure all yuca is incorporated. Spoon the dough onto a large piece of parchment paper and roll it out to about ¼ to ⅓ inch (6 to 8 mm) thick. Use a pizza cutter to slice the dough into 3 x 3-inch (7.5 x 7.5 cm) squares.

Heat the frying oil in a saucepan over high heat. Fry the squares in small batches until crispy on both sides. They may puff while frying but will not be as air-filled as the original version. Dust with powdered stevia or tapioca starch (cosmetic only) or drizzle with honey and serve warm!

BLACK-EYED SUSANS

(GRAIN-, DAIRY-, EGG-, SOY-, NIGHTSHADE-FREE)

I remember these cookies from a local grocery store growing up. We'd bring them home by the dozen and they'd be gone before you could blink. I kept the sweeteners to a minimum here and omitted the white flour, of course, but the flavor is still reminiscent of childhood and is decadent to boot! To make your own cashew meal, grind whole cashews in a food processor, pulsing until a fine powder; it is not necessary to purchase ready-made cashew meal.

YIELD: 8 SERVINGS

FOR THE COOKIES

1 cup (120 g) cashew meal

1 cup (120 g) almond flour

4 tsp (20 ml) pure maple syrup

2 tbsp (30 ml) organic palm shortening

½ tsp pure vanilla extract

¼ tsp salt

½ tsp baking soda

FOR THE FILLING

¼ cup (38 g) dairy- and soy-free dark chocolate chips

2 tbsp (30 ml) full-fat coconut milk

2 tbsp (30 ml) palm shortening

Preheat the oven to 350°F (180°C, or gas mark 4).

To make the cookies, combine all the ingredients in a blender or food processor. Blend until well combined. Roll 1 tablespoon (15 g) of dough into a ball, place on a parchment-lined baking sheet and press the ball of dough in the center, creating a reservoir to hold the filling. Repeat with the remaining dough. Bake for 10 minutes, remove the cookies carefully from the oven and allow them to cool for 5–10 minutes. You might need to press slightly on the centers of the cookies if they filled in or puffed up while baking.

To make the filling, melt the chocolate chips and coconut milk in a small saucepan over medium heat for about 4 minutes, stirring continually. Be careful not to burn the chocolate, so remove it from the heat as soon as it is melted and the coconut milk is incorporated well. Add the shortening and stir well. Allow to cool slightly so it can firm up, about 5 minutes.

Place the filling in a pastry bag (or a sandwich bag with the tip cut off) and pipe into the centers of the cookies. You'll want to pipe about 1 teaspoon (5 g) per cookie. Serve right away or store in an airtight container.

★ SEE PAGE 136 FOR IMAGE.

TRES LECHES CAKE

(GRAIN-, DAIRY-, SOY-, NIGHTSHADE-FREE)

Tres leches literally translates to "three milks," though in reality the interpretation is more along the lines of "Can I please eat this every day for the rest of my life?" It is one of the most memorable desserts around, and while the three milks chosen for this version are all dairy-free, they still deliver the same incredible richness of the original.

YIELD: 8 SERVINGS

FOR THE CAKE

½ cup (60 g) coconut flour

½ cup (120 ml) coconut oil, melted

½ tsp baking soda

¼ cup (60 ml) pure maple syrup

2 tsp (10 ml) pure Madagascar vanilla extract

¼ tsp sea salt

5 pastured eggs

FOR THE MILKS

½ cup (120 ml) full-fat coconut milk

¼ cup (60 ml) cashew or almond milk

¼ cup (60 ml) flax milk

3 tbsp (45 ml) pure maple syrup

FOR SERVING

Coconut Whipped Cream (page 159)

Ground cinnamon (optional)

Sliced strawberries (optional)

Preheat the oven to 350°F (180°C, or gas mark 4).

To make the cake, combine all the cake ingredients in a blender and pulse or blend on low until well combined. The batter will be fairly runny. Pour the cake batter into a small, 6-cup (1.5 L) greased glass casserole dish; 8 x 6 inches (20 x 15 cm) works well. Bake for 25–30 minutes, or until a toothpick inserted into the center comes out clean and the cake is firm but springy.

To make the milks, while the cake is baking, whisk together the three milks and maple syrup in a small mixing bowl. Note: If you'd rather prepare a nut-free recipe, omit the cashew/almond milk and replace with either additional coconut milk or flax milk.

Once the cake is finished baking, carefully remove from the oven and pierce it with a fork 15–20 times. Pour the milk mixture over the aerated cake and refrigerate until the cake absorbs most of the liquid and is chilled.

Once the cake is chilled, remove from the refrigerator and spread the Coconut Whipped Cream over the top. Slice and serve. Optionally, you may garnish with a dash of cinnamon on top or fresh sliced strawberries.

WET YOUR WHISTLE

Quenching your thirst has never been so inviting! Southern beverages are packed with personality and a splash of sweetness, just like those serving them. These are all made with whole food ingredients and flavored without refined sugar, so rest assured: these are all naturally as sweet as the Southern soul who prepares them!

If you've never had Watermelon + Cilantro Agua Fresca (page 180), New Orleans Café au Lait (page 176) or Mexican Hot Chocolate (page 179), these are all awaiting your taste buds here. Sparkling Ginger Peach Punch (page 181) sound like your style? No problem! Explore the flavors and sass of the South right here while you sip on these!

LIP SMACKIN' LEMONADE

(GRAIN-, DAIRY-, NUT-, EGG-, SOY-, NIGHTSHADE-FREE)

Have you ever read the label on store-bought powdered lemonade mix? There are a ton of ingredients and not one of them is from real lemons! This lemonade recipe will make you pucker up for more and is made with only a handful of whole food ingredients.

YIELD: 10 SERVINGS

10 cups (2350 ml) water or sparkling mineral water

4 large lemons

30 drops lemon-flavored stevia drops or ¼ cup (60 ml) local raw honey

5 tbsp (40 g) grass-fed gelatin (optional)

Fill your pitcher or dispenser with the water. Slice the lemons and squeeze into the water. Add the lemon-flavored stevia and stir. Alternatively, local raw honey can be used to replace the stevia; just stir it in until it dissolves. The gelatin can be added at this time as well, stirring until incorporated. To make the lemonade extra tart, add more lemons. Serve right away or store in the refrigerator for up to a week.

NATURALLY SWEETENED SWEET TEA

(GRAIN-, DAIRY-, EGG-, NUT-, SOY-, NIGHTSHADE-FREE)

If you think the image of Southerners sitting on their front stoops drinking sweet tea by the gallon is a stereotype, you might be right. But it isn't a stretch by much. From Georgia to Texas, sweet tea is a cherished commodity; it also has enough sugar to last you from here 'til next Thursday. This version uses stevia to keep things naturally sweet.

YIELD: 8 SERVINGS

8 cups (1880 ml) water

8 black tea bags

60 drops liquid stevia or local honey to taste

Fresh squeezed lemon juice to taste

Ice cubes (optional)

Pour the water into a large saucepan over high heat, drop in the tea bags and allow to simmer for 5 minutes (or longer if you prefer a stronger tea). Remove from the heat and remove the tea bags. Add the stevia drops or honey and lemon juice to taste and stir. Refrigerate or add ice cubes to chill the tea. Can't stand watered-down tea? Freeze the sweet tea in an ice cube tray and your tea will stay bold and flavorful!

CITRUS BERRY SMOOTHIE

(GRAIN-, EGG-, DAIRY-, NUT-, SOY-, NIGHTSHADE-FREE)

What's a person to do on a scorching Southern summer day when it's just too darn hot to crank an oven? Make a delicious, nutrient-dense smoothie, of course! This one includes spinach and berries for a cool treat that is jam-packed with goodness!

YIELD: 2 SERVINGS

---

1 cup (70 g) organic baby spinach

1 cup (150 g) frozen organic mixed berries

1 cup (235 ml) freshly squeezed orange juice

2 tbsp (16 g) grass-fed gelatin (optional)

It doesn't get any easier than this! Combine all the ingredients in a blender and puree until there are no fruit chunks remaining. You can adjust the thickness by adding a little extra juice or water for a thinner consistency. Prefer less sugar? Substitute ½ cup (120 ml) sparkling water for ½ cup (120 ml) of the orange juice.

NEW ORLEANS CAFÉ AU LAIT

(GRAIN-, DAIRY-, NUT-, EGG-, SOY-, NIGHTSHADE-FREE)

If you've ever been to New Orleans, you know that it is famous for Bourbon Street, Cajun fare and café au lait with hot beignets, right out of the fryer. There is just something about that chicory root brewed into the coffee that is both distinct and incredibly comforting. Now you can enjoy that comfort in your own home with this deliciously rich dairy-free version! This recipe makes a single serving, but if more is desired, simply multiply the coffee and chicory quantities by the number of cups you'd like to prepare.

YIELD: 1 SERVING

1 tbsp (15 ml) organic high-quality coffee grounds

1 tsp (3 g) ground chicory root

1 cup (235 ml) water

¼–½ cup (60–120 ml) full-fat coconut milk, almond milk or flax milk

Coconut sugar, stevia or maple sugar (optional)

In your coffee maker of choice, brew the ground coffee and chicory root with the water. After brewing, add the milk and sweetener, if desired.

MEXICAN HOT CHOCOLATE

(GRAIN-, EGG-, DAIRY-, NUT-, SOY-FREE)

In Texas, natives know this sassy hot chocolate well, and those newer to the Lone Star State catch on quickly. Paired with cinnamon, nutmeg and a pinch of cayenne, it is sure to warm up even the coldest cowboys (and girls)!

YIELD: 3 SERVINGS

3 cups (705 ml) flax milk, almond milk or coconut milk

4 tsp (12 g) organic cocoa powder

⅛ tsp ground cinnamon

⅛ tsp ground nutmeg

2 tbsp (24 g) coconut palm sugar

10 drops chocolate-flavored stevia

FOR SERVING

Pinch of cayenne pepper (optional)

Coconut Whipped Cream (page 159, optional)

In a medium-size saucepan, heat the milk over medium heat, then add in the cocoa powder, cinnamon, nutmeg, sugar and stevia, whisking continually until well incorporated, about 1 minute. Bring the hot chocolate to a brief simmer, approximately 2 more minutes, and then remove from the heat and serve right away. Top with the Coconut Whipped Cream for a special treat!

WATERMELON +
CILANTRO AGUA FRESCA

(GRAIN-, EGG-, DAIRY-, NUT-, NIGHTSHADE-FREE)

Who wants to wet their whistle with plain ol' ice water? This agua fresca combines cool,
sweet watermelon with a hint of cilantro. When it's as hot out as blue blazes,
this refreshing drink is as delicious as it is hydrating!

YIELD: 6 SERVINGS

---

2 lbs (908 g) chopped and seeded
watermelon

3 tbsp (45 ml) local raw honey

1 cup (235 ml) water

¼ cup (15 g) fresh cilantro, for garnish

Place the watermelon, honey and water in a blender and blend on high until smooth.
Pour the mixture over a strainer to filter out any residual seeds. Divide among 6 glasses
and garnish with a sprig or two of cilantro. To take it up a notch, you can also muddle
the cilantro in the bottom of each glass before pouring the agua fresca over the top.

SPARKLING GINGER PEACH PUNCH

(GRAIN-, DAIRY-, NUT-, EGG-, NIGHTSHADE-FREE)

Traditional Southern punch can be sickeningly sweet and spike blood sugar faster than a prairie fire with a tail wind! This punch is just as refreshing but won't leave you with a sugar crash.

YIELD: 4 SERVINGS

1 lb (454 g) peach slices

3 tbsp (45 ml) pure maple syrup

½ tsp ground ginger

4 cups (940 ml) sparkling water

Ice

In a blender, puree the peaches, maple syrup and ginger, making sure not to leave any chunks behind. Spoon the peach puree into the bottom of a large pitcher. Pour the sparkling water over the top, stir gently and serve right away, over ice, to prevent loss of carbonation.

VIRGIN MOJITO

(GRAIN-, EGG-, DAIRY-, NUT-, NIGHTSHADE-FREE)

This mojito is served up without the hangover! Delicious and refreshing, the cool mint and
the subtle sweetness from the honey make this the perfect summer spritzer!

YIELD: 1 SERVING

10 fresh mint leaves

Juice from 2 small limes

2 tsp (10 ml) local raw honey

½ cup (75 g) crushed ice

¾ cup (180 ml) sparkling mineral water

In a glass, muddle (crush) the mint, lime juice and honey. Add the crushed ice and then
pour the sparkling mineral water over the ice. Stir slightly and serve!

★ SEE PAGE 170 FOR IMAGE.

LEMON + BLACKBERRY SPARKLER

(GRAIN-, DAIRY-, EGG-, NUT-, NIGHTSHADE-FREE)

Cool off on a hot day with this sparkler, perfect for sippin' on the front porch, poolside or anywhere really! Local raw honey sweetens this spritzer for a sparkling drink that's as purty as it is tasty!

YIELD: 4 SERVINGS

6 oz (170 g) blackberries

2 tbsp (30 ml) local raw honey

Juice of 3 large lemons, plus wedges for garnish

4 cups (940 ml) sparkling water

Puree the blackberries in a blender and then press the puree through a mesh sieve or strainer. Return the strained puree to the blender and add the honey and lemon juice. Blend once more until the ingredients are mixed well. Pour the mixture into a large pitcher and add the sparkling water. Stir and serve with a lemon wedge to garnish.

ALL ABOUT YUCA, Y'ALL

If you've followed *Predominantly Paleo* for a while, it's no secret that yuca has quickly become a fascination of mine! If you are giving up grains yet want to keep Tex-Mex and other favorite foods alive, yuca is a fantastic option that is not only versatile, but also takes on multiple textures and flavors.

In other parts of the world, yuca root, also known as cassava, is a staple food: cheap, filling and easy to acquire. Here in the U.S., less is known about the root, and when it is prepared, as with many Latin dishes, it is typically made similarly to French fries. Once I started realizing all of its majestic properties, I quickly fell in love.

In this chapter, you will find recipes for tortilla chips, soft tortillas and tostadas, all yuca based, as well as some frequently asked questions on yuca dough preparation.

PLEASE NOTE: Yuca can take some time and effort to prepare, but once you have mastered the process, it can be a great alternative to its grain-laden counterparts! Please read through these questions and answers and the full set of instructions if you are new to yuca. I wrote this chapter so that it might take some of the guesswork out of working with this magical tuber!

FREQUENTLY ASKED QUESTIONS

1. WHERE CAN I FIND YUCA?

You can find yuca at your mainstream grocery store in the fresh produce section near the papayas, mangos and plantains. If your local store does not carry it, speak with the produce manager and request they order it for you. It is also sometimes available in the frozen section in a 5-pound (2.3 kg) bag and it works beautifully! If your main grocery doesn't have it, check with Latin and Asian markets or health food stores.

2. WHAT IS THE BEST WAY TO GET THE THICK SKIN (TREE BARK) OFF?

You may use a knife and cutting board or you may use a vegetable peeler. I personally have a much easier time peeling it with a vegetable peeler.

3. IF PURCHASED IN BULK CAN YOU CUT AND FREEZE IT FOR LATER?

Yes!

4. HOW LONG DOES THE YUCA ROOT STAY FRESH IN THE FRIDGE?

I leave mine unrefrigerated and if purchased fresh it can last up to 2 weeks. In the fridge, I'd imagine about the same, maybe slightly longer, but it will depend on how fresh the root was when purchased.

5. IS THE FROZEN YUCA ACCEPTABLE?

Yes! I use it and have had great success with it.

6. HOW LONG CAN I KEEP YUCA DOUGH IN THE FRIDGE?

No more than 3 or 4 days, and it must not be exposed to air or it will harden.

7. IS YUCA THE SAME AS YUCCA?

No, yucca is an ornamental-looking plant that supposedly has edible parts, but it is not the same as the yuca root, which is also known as cassava.

8. WHY IS MY DOUGH STILL STICKY?

Tips for creating a less sticky dough: cut large pieces to boil, boil only until fork-tender, allow to cool and air dry slightly before blending, add coconut flour until it is less sticky (usually only needing 1–2 tablespoons [8–16 g]) and allow to also cool before trying to work with the dough (post blending). Sometimes you will get a root that seems overripe and extra sticky. It happens.

9. IS YUCA LOW CARB?

No, it's not. It is definitely a good starch for many and is versatile, but is not low carb.

10. IS YUCA THE SAME AS TAPIOCA?

Yes and no. Tapioca is derived from yuca but is just the starch component. I think of it as potato flour vs. potato starch. They start from the same place but vary in their properties in cooking.

11. DOES IT COOK LIKE A POTATO?

In some ways, yes. I love using it in place of potatoes in some recipes, especially for those who cannot tolerate nightshades.

12. ARE THE TOXINS IN THE YUCA SKIN DANGEROUS?

The toxins are primarily in the skin and are taken care of by stripping the skin off thoroughly and by cooking thoroughly, which is accomplished through the boiling, baking and frying process.

13. HOW CAN I PREVENT OVERHEATING MY BLENDER OR FOOD PROCESSOR?

Start by increasing the speed from low to higher over the course of a few minutes. Be sure to use your tamper (if your appliance has one) quickly and assertively to make sure the yuca chunks get shoved into the blades. You can also blend in small batches so as to not overload your machine.

14. DO I NEED TO HAVE A HEAVY-DUTY BLENDER OR FOOD PROCESSOR TO MAKE YUCA DOUGH?

Yuca is a very dense, fibrous root. If you do not have a machine with a sturdy motor to handle processing it, you will likely be disappointed in the results. Even with a heavy-duty blender, it is possible to overheat the motor if precautions are not taken, so it is best to have a machine that is properly equipped. Alternatively you can grate the yuca and blend more easily, though the prep work is a bit longer.

BASIC YUCA DOUGH RECIPES

TORTILLA CHIPS

YIELD: 3 SERVINGS

2 lbs (908 g) peeled and coarsely chopped yuca root

2 tbsp (30 ml) avocado or coconut oil

1 tsp (3 g) garlic sea salt

2 tbsp (16 g) coconut flour, as needed (optional)

Bring a large stockpot filled halfway with water to a boil over high heat, add the peeled yuca root and cook for 25 minutes, or until you can pierce it easily. Drain the water and remove from the stockpot. Transfer to a cutting board. Remove the fibrous core from the center of the yuca once cool enough to handle.

Transfer the pieces to a sturdy blender (preferably with a tamper) or a food processor once they have cooled slightly. Add the oil and garlic sea salt and turn on your machine from low to high, gradually increasing the speed. If you are using a heavy-duty blender, be sure to use the tamper to really press the yuca down into the blade. This will help remove any chunks and give you a nice workable dough. Let cool.

While the dough is cooling, preheat the oven to 375°F (190°C, or gas mark 5).

Use a spoon to empty the blender or food processor onto a piece of parchment paper. If the dough is still sticky, allow it to cool more or add the optional coconut flour 1 tablespoon (8 g) at a time until the dough is less sticky. Place another piece of parchment paper on top of the dough and roll out until it is about ¼ inch (6 mm) thick. Transfer the bottom parchment and dough to a large baking sheet. Use a pizza cutter to score triangle shapes in your dough.

Bake for 30 minutes and then remove from the oven to test the crispiness. If more baking time is needed, you may return the chips to the oven for an additional 10–15 minutes, depending on the desired texture. Once optimal crispness is achieved, remove from the oven and break the chips apart where they were scored with the pizza cutter.

TOSTADAS

YIELD: 6 TOSTADAS

---

1 recipe Tortilla Chips dough (page 187)

Preheat the oven to 375°F (190°C, or gas mark 5).

Divide the dough into 6 pieces and roll them flat between two pieces of parchment paper. Alternatively, you may press out the tostada by hand, making a round disk approximately ⅛ inch (6 mm) thick. Bake the tostadas on a parchment-lined baking sheet in batches, depending on what your baking sheet can accommodate, for about 30 minutes, until all 6 tostadas are done. As oven temperatures can vary, watch the tostadas while they bake; they are ready once they are nicely browned and crisped. Optionally, you can flip them over after 15 minutes but this is not a required step. If desired, the tostados can be pan fried in a teaspoon (5 ml) of oil over high heat for a minute or so for added crispness. If not using right away, they may be stored in the freezer and toasted up as needed.

TACO SHELLS

YIELD: 8 TACO SHELLS

---

1 recipe Tortilla dough (page 189)

Preheat the oven to 350°F (180°C, or gas mark 4).

On a parchment-lined work surface, roll out a handful of dough to form a tortilla about ⅛ inch (3 mm) thick. Repeat to make 8 tortillas. Place on parchment-lined baking sheets.

Bake for 10–15 minutes, or until the tortillas are set but not completely cooked. Remove the baking sheet from the oven and carefully fold the tortillas over a taco rack. If they crack at the seam, the dough easily presses back together by hand if not overcooked. This is why cooking times are crucial. Alternatively, you can fold the par-baked tortillas over the grates on the center oven rack. Bake for another 10–20 minutes, or until the taco shells are crisped and nicely browned. Watch them to prevent burning.

TORTILLAS

YIELD: 8 TORTILLAS

2 lbs (908 g) peeled and coarsely chopped yuca root

1 ripe plantain

¼ cup (60 ml) avocado oil

1 tsp (3 g) garlic sea salt

Preheat the oven to 350°F (180°C, or gas mark 4).

Bring a large stockpot filled halfway with water to a boil over high heat, add the peeled yuca root and cook for 25 minutes, or until you can pierce it easily with a fork. Drain the water and remove yuca from the stockpot. Transfer to a cutting board. Remove the fibrous core from the center of the yuca once cool enough to handle. Allow the cooked yuca to air-dry and cool slightly by letting it sit for about 10 minutes. This will help some of the moisture evaporate so the dough is not too sticky when you blend it.

Combine the cooked yuca, plantain, oil and salt in a blender or food processor, preferably one with a tamper so that you can coerce the bigger chunks down into the blades. Blend until pureed (the mixture will be thick, like dough).

On a parchment-lined work surface, roll out a handful of dough to form a tortilla about ⅛ inch (3 mm) thick. Repeat to make 8 tortillas. Place on parchment-lined baking sheets.

Bake for 10 minutes on one side, then remove from the oven, flip the tortillas over and bake for another 5–10 minutes, or until the tortillas are cooked through (baking time will depend on how thick your tortillas are). Once cooked they will be slightly crisped on the edges and nice and pliable in the center. Overcooking them will result in more of a tostada, which is crispier throughout.

ACKNOWLEDGMENTS

★ ★ ★

This book was a labor of love, with the labor weighing in as heavily as the love some days. I had fears before committing to this endeavor because I doubted my ability to pull off such a feat while still healing. Without my team of supporters, I never would have had the courage.

To Ben, my rock, for believing in my abilities and mostly for cleaning up the kitchen after a long day of my "creations," even though you had just worked a 12-hour day yourself. Love you forever.

To Mom, for always being my cheerleader regardless of my latest (and ever-changing) project. To Pop, for being the grounded one and for assuring me that it would be great, even though the word "Paleo" might have sounded like some sort of South American ritual dance.

To my three littles: Noah, Sadie and Stella, who were always willing to try new recipes, even the ones that weren't my best (and no, those didn't make the book).

To Shauna, one of my oldest childhood friends, who enthusiastically stayed up late texting ideas for the table of contents before I even had a book deal or a recipe written.

To Blair, my best military friend, who never had a doubt that I could somehow pull this feat off, despite knowing my challenges. Or, at least in being a great friend, kept her doubts to herself!

To Stacy, for taking me under your wing and showing me the way. Thanks for teaching me that there is enough success to go around, and for taking the time to write my foreword. Your influence has been invaluable.

And a heartfelt thanks to Page Street Publishing, for taking the gamble on this Lone Star girl. This book literally would not exist without y'all!

To all of my loyal readers, thank you for your enthusiasm and for appreciating the efforts poured into this work.

ABOUT THE AUTHOR

★ ★ ★

JENNIFER ROBINS is the voice and whole foodist behind the popular food blog Predominantly Paleo. After being diagnosed with several autoimmune conditions and chronic infections, including Lyme disease, Jennifer became gravely ill and mostly housebound. When traditional medical treatments failed to help, Jennifer turned to food for healing. Removing grain, dairy and refined sugars and eating "predominantly Paleo," she started reclaiming her life, one whole food at a time. As a wife and mother of three, Jennifer hopes to instill healthy habits in her children now in hopes of creating wellness for a lifetime.

INDEX